A Touch of Treason

A TOUCH OF TREASON

Ian R Hamilton QC

LOCHAR PUBLISHING • MOFFAT • SCOTLAND

To the memory of my father

Fold of value in the world west from Greece
Over whom it has been our duty to keep guard
Have we slept on our watch?

From *Lament for the Great Music*
by Hugh MacDiarmid

© Ian Hamilton 1990
Published by Lochar Publishing Limited
MOFFAT

This edition published September 1990
Reprinted January 1991

British Library Cataloguing in Publication Data
Hamilton, Ian *1925 –*
    A touch of treason
    1. Scotland. Law. Biographies
    I. Title
    344.110092

ISBN 0–948403–45–4

Typeset in 11pt on 13pt Palatino by Dumfries ITeC
and printed in Great Britain by BPCC Wheaton's Ltd, Exeter.

CONTENTS

FOREWORD

Herein is fascinating reading, enthralling, challenging, controversial indeed but humerous also, the life, doings, thoughts, beliefs successes and failures of a very positive and human character. Ian Hamilton, whom I have known for forty years, is a man who has always thought deeply, felt deeply, and acted upon his conclusions and findings, vehemently, courageously, at whatever cost to himself – unlike most of us.

You will not agree with all he writes here but that is no small part of the drama and gripping quality of this book. Ian, as well as being an eminent Queen's Counsel (are all QC's eminent?) is a born storyteller, which perhaps had something to do with his career as an advocate also. But, as you will learn, he does not confine his persuasive powers to the law-courts.

I could comment endlessly on this autobiography, but will not. It speaks for itself, strongly, pungently, wittily. Its writer and I disagree on sundry subjects – worship and church going, for one; the royal house's position for another (although I agree that the Numeral is wrong for Scotland; indeed I sat through the court hearing on that renowned case). As for the Stone of Destiny, Ian admits that the stone may indeed not be the real one, although he went to so much trouble to abstract it from Westminster Abbey in 1950; I however, have no doubts that this one is a 700-year-old fake, which Edward, Hammer of the Scots, was palmed of with in 1296, the true *Lia Faill* being described by the ancient chroniclers as very different, ornate, chair-height, indeed Scotland's Marble Chair. Unlike Ian, I had nothing to do with the taking of the London stone, only some small part in helping to bring it to light again, in dignified fashion, at Arbroath Abbey, where Scotland's great Declaration of Independence was signed. An old and controversial story, but its fascination does not fade. Where is the true Stone of Destiny now?

6

However, that episode is a very small, but not unimportant, chapter of this exciting book. Scotland itself is the theme, the passion of it – but this is not to suggest that it will not almost equally intrigue, concern and amuse English and overseas readers. Especially in this day and age when we have seen such an upsurge of national consciousness and democratic assertion. Read it – and it will give you food for thought, debate, exasperation, joy – and many a chuckle.

Nigel Tranter

1 Boy at Arms

JUST BEFORE he was hanged, one of my ancestors asked his accusers to change the hemp rope for a silk one. Hemp, he explained was rough on the neck. Another of the family, my grandmother's great-uncle Tom, called publicly for the prosecution for cowardice of his commanding officer. It nearly ended his career. Each brave man was asserting the prime right of the individual to condemn those jacks in office who owe their place to birth, mediocrity and a noisy support for the *status quo*. Scotland is still full of them. My hanged ancestor has no known grave, but his monument is the Great Hall in Stirling Castle which he designed. Grandmother's great-uncle Tom is buried in Westminster Abbey where he must be uncomfortable in the company he keeps. There will be fun there on the great day of judgment when he rises, looks about him and picks a fight. My bet is that he will be one of the few who come out of the Abbey alive. Grandmother's great-uncle Tom was a survivor.

Such curious blood-lines were never traceable in our family home in Paisley. Hangings were for others, and so was Westminster Abbey. My father was a tailor. His shop was not in the grand mould, but something which had strayed away from Victorian times and got lost in a back street tenement. He called himself a merchant tailor and never stocked a ready-made suit in his life. He would as soon have run a massage parlour. With a mouth full of pins, he measured his customers and pinned patterns and bits of cloth to them, until he had built up a suit as enduring as a Clyde-built ship. He was respected by his peers and became President of the Federation of Merchant Tailors. They gave him a gold chain of office to prove it. Many years later it was stolen, recovered, and passed up to me where I sat on the bench as a sheriff. I glanced down and saw my father's name engraved on a little

9

gold medallion. It was like holding his tombstone in my hand.

A sheriff's life is a somewhat narrow and unadventurous one, but not as narrow as that of a tailor's son in Paisley. Oh that was narrow, narrow, and nothing was more narrow than our religious upbringing. My elder brother and I were forced to attend every Sunday along with our parents at the local Church of Scotland, where my father was Session Clerk. At first the pews were so high that my feet did not reach to the floor, and I could amuse myself by swinging my heels together during the sermon, a pastime fascinating to a little boy, but one much disapproved of. Later, when my legs had grown longer there was nothing for it but to listen to the sermons. My whole future life was shaped by these sermons. Gradually it dawned on me that they were a load of rubbish. Reading a chapter of the Bible every night gave me a familiarity with the sources of religion, and my dissent was suppressed but very real. There must be few institutions on earth more lacking in Christian charity than that Church of Scotland, and none more out of touch with life. By the time puberty had arrived I had settled into an amiable agnosticism, which has alternated ever since with an occasional burst of enthusiastic ætheism. If there is an omnipotent God he is of fathomless wickedness and I am against him.

This departure from the faith of my forefathers has a simple explanation. Book-burners are right. Put an enquiring child in a house with a shelf of books which include Darwin, Carlyle, and Shaw, and make him also listen to a Church of Scotland minister and something is bound to happen. It did. My father believed devoutly in God, and would be shocked by my views, but he was devoutly in two minds, each mind unwaveringly contradictory of the other. He believed as firmly in Noah's Ark as he did in the *Origin of Species*. He preserved his sanity by never letting one mind argue with the other. This trick leads to inconsistency, which is better than dogma and so long as I lived under his roof I went along with him. Nowadays my only contact with the Church of Scotland is at the start of each criminal circuit, when a minister is brought along to pray for the Queen, the judge, us, and anything else he can think of except the poor wretch in the dock. I attend to listen to these words in wonderment.

Such a mentally divisive, and indeed perplexing upbringing plagued my schooldays. My parents sent me to the John Neilson Institution, a modest fee-paying Paisley school where the other children were of like families to my own. This kept me from meeting poorer children who might debase my accent by teaching me the language of Henryson and Lindsay and Fergusson and Dunbar, and of a line of kings and commoners stretching back a thousand years. Speaking proper was as important as behaving proper. Like every schoolboy I tried to conform and my first communion with authority came unasked. It was wartime. France had fallen, and there was an exuberance in the land as though we had just won a great victory, yet it was a grim exuberance, very much mixed with fear. The Battle of Britain was being fought and we expected the enemy to make a landing any day. I made a pike from a bread-knife lashed to an ash-pole and waited for them. Anyone who laughs should speak to a Czech or a Pole or a Russian and read some history. It was in this time of bravery for the whole British peoples that we were suddenly told that the King and Queen were to pass along a road near the school and that we were all to go there to line the route and cheer. My reaction was predictable. What had the House of Windsor to do with Paisley, or Paisley with the House of Windsor? I got on my bike and went home. Liberty to cheer means liberty not to cheer, and conscription is offensive to every free man. I was fourteen years of age.

Some of my fellows must have told of my absence, because scarcely every child can have been counted. In any event I was missed. Being hauled before the school introduced me to that feeling which is the stock in trade of every advocate who

11

stands between his client and the baying of the mob. It is a hell-mend-you-I-will-die for this feeling. So it felt to me then and so it feels to me still, the great power of being alone. Looking back it is clear that the school did not know how to handle such a mutiny, but that did not deter them from publicly branding me an anarchist and a communist. An eager exploration of these two political labels disclosed the fact that they were mutually exclusive, and that very recently their adherents had been killing one another in Spain. This discovery put me one up on my teachers and when it was duly communicated to my history mistress war broke out. As in all wars there were no winners; unlike real wars the combatants enjoyed themselves.

This war was probably the first fluttering of my fluffy wings because after that learning became more fun. What had been a slog became an enquiry, and I had to work more diligently to keep my end up. I did not know it but I was competing against myself, which is the best competition of all. The John Neilson gave a sound grounding in the subjects which even yet are considered part of a liberal education, but we were never taught a morsel of Scottish history. This gap in the curriculum can only have been a deliberate attempt to assimilate us young Scots into an English mould, a second class English mould, because we could never quite identify with a people who were not us. York and Lancaster were far away places in a far away country, and Runnymede might have been a cold in the head for all we cared, and for all Magna Carta has done for humanity we might have been right. Most lost interest. No one ever told us that under our very feet there had been a camp of the Roman legions who had come to attempt to conquer us and been turned back by our own flesh and blood bearing only arms like the very pike I had made to kill Germans. We were told that Julius Caesar had come because he liked oysters.

It was left to my family to fill the gap. When that great patriot Fletcher of Saltoun said that it did not matter who made the laws of the country so long as we still make the songs, perhaps he was only overstating a fundamental truth. We had no radio and of course there was no television. At family gatherings we sang round the piano and apart from 'Men of Harlech' the songs were all Scottish songs. They stated principles and raised questions and when my mother put me to bed she answered these questions by telling me of Black Agnes dusting Dunbar Castle walls as the English bombarded it with their engines of war, and then waving her duster at them, which was a fine thing to do. She also told me of the Good Lord James, and hushed me to sleep with, 'Hush ye hush ye dinna fret ye, Jamie Douglas wilna get ye'. From the stories she told of him he became one of my heroes, and he still occupies a place in my pantheon with the great Montrose.

The mystery is where my mother got these stories. They did not come from any book. *Scots Tales of a Grandfather* was in the house, but my mother never put her nose into anything more edifying than *The People's Friend*, of which I was also at that time an aficionado. She had never had much education. The stories she told me must have been handed down to her by her mother and so on back to the events themselves. They were true folk memories. History sometimes runs underground, and my father tapped the same well. His great friend was John Morrison, then Paisley Town Clerk. Father and John Morrison were instrumental in getting the rather ugly cairn erected which still stands between Paisley and Renfrew to mark the spot where the pregnant Princess Marjorie was thrown from her horse and gave birth. That child was the first of the Stewart dynasty, ancestor of the present Queen. If anyone had called father and Mr Morrison Scottish Nationalists they would have sued.

Humble people that they were there was a quality about my parents that made me feel that wherever they stood was the right of the line, and I am not talking about politics. My father was never anything but his own man. He would have been unemployable by anyone else, just as I have been. The only job he ever had was that of a special constable during the war years. Also like me he was far too wee to get into a police uniform so he had to go on foot-patrol in civvies. He never arrested anyone. Despite his height he had such a dignity about him that a word from him was probably heeded. He had been Scottish champion miler in his day and had run against Eric Liddell, whom he greatly admired long before the film *Chariots of Fire* made him famous. They had run together in some cross-country race in which they were both trailing the field. Competitors in front had partly knocked down the brush-wood fence and others were taking advantage of this gap as they were entitled to do. Eric Liddell disdained the advantage and swerved to the side and jumped the full fence itself, and so did my father. He never drew any moral from that story, and it is retold here with pride. While my father was walking the blacked-out streets as a policeman my mother was organising the local sector of the A R P. They were both over fifty years of age.

Among their great friends was the family over the garden wall. The man had a little grocery shop in a slum district in Paisley and the wife ran a paper shop. As a family they were as like as two peas to our own. Their son became a Court of Session judge, and in later years I was often to have the privilege of appearing before him. It is no insult to the judiciary to say that had it not been for the songs and stories of my childhood I might have ended up like him. These songs and stories, and many of the ideas in my father's books wormed away in my head and by my mid teens they had quite taken over. Judges are the pillars of the community, and twentieth century Scotland needs pulling down and rebuilding rather than propping up.

This view was fortified by the last two years of my education. My father had not had much of a schooling himself. He was denied a university education when his father was killed in a bicycling accident, and he had to set to to support his mother and brothers and sister. He was determined to do better by his own family. He sent my brother to Allan Glen's School in Glasgow, and in due course I followed. Two years for each of us was all he could afford. Allan Glen's was a wonderful school. It had a tendency to science and taught mathematics, physics and dynamics to a high standard. The school could have been for me a bleak desert had it not been for David Strachan who was head of the English department and who doubled as history master it being wartime. The way he taught illuminated the whole curriculum.

It was not just the school which raised my horizons and put me into what seemed then to be big sky country. Having a season ticket on the train to Glasgow was an education in itself. Even in wartime Glasgow there were theatres and concerts. Franz Lehar and Strauss were frequently sung in the most extravagant costume. God knows how they were financed. There were also political meetings, mainly of the hard left, held in the most dingy of halls smelling of people and varnish to which I crept and wondered. Revolution was on the breath of all the speakers, but to be truthful they seemed a dingy lot to me.

Two exceptions come readily to mind. They are Guy Aldred and John Taylor Caldwell. I had thought that these people were forgotten and had meant to pay a lonely tribute to them. John Caldwell has recently published a biography of Guy Aldred of whom he was a disciple, so the memory is refreshed. Mine needs no refreshing. Guy Aldred was an Englishman who did us the great honour of settling among us in Glasgow. He espoused every unpopular cause from basic Christianity to anarchism, and was jailed more often for sedition and like crimes than any other political figure this century. He was even jailed for advocating birth control and women's lib. The establishment loathed him, but gradually the police came to admire him for the work he did among the destitute in

A Touch of Treason

Glasgow. When the Communists tried to get him interned during the war it is said that Churchill himself stepped in and would not have it. In a ruinous little shop in George Street, not far from the school he printed pamphlets and from it he published all manner of wild literature, and gave advice freely to anyone in need.

One day in their shop John Caldwell and Guy Aldred were standing watching, while I was thumbing over some pamphlets. One of them spoke to me.

'I hope they're not teaching you religion in that fancy school of yours up the hill,' he said.

To which I replied, 'Voltaire says that if no God exists it will be necessary to invent one.' Then we fell to, myself on the side of God. He needed a better advocate against these two.

Often in the years to come that argument in that ruinous shop in a slum street in Glasgow was to come back to refresh me. It gave me far more than my classes in philosophy at Glasgow University. There is a sort of innocence about a schoolboy, and he very easily sees through humbug. Guy Aldred and John Caldwell were the first people who took my arguments seriously enough to answer them seriously. Each man, unless he follows the herd takes his own lonely road. My own conclusions were reached without their help, but their very way of life confirmed me in the view that the lonely road is the only one. They were like characters out of *The Pilgrim's Progress*. When the trumpets sounded on the other side for Guy Aldred in 1963 he had only ninepence in his pocket. A whole city suddenly realised what it had lost and mourned his passing.

My nodding acquaintance with these two did not lead to further exchanges. Time and circumstance were pushing me into myself. In a few months my age group would have to register for military service. This was a perfectly simple process, and should have offered no difficulties. I wanted to be a fighter pilot and from a very early age I had assumed that I would take part in the war, survive, and become a hero. This was exactly what the Government also wanted, and my ambition was a direct response to all the conditioning which has gone on since ever there were wars to be fought and young men to fight them. Now I was not so sure. Allan Glen's had opened my mind, already receptive to new ideas, and my reading had gone far beyond my father's bookshelves. I had formed the view, which has never left me, that to be a good soldier one must be an imbecile, that war is fought for the conscientious objectors, and that it is through them, and not through warriors that civilisation will advance. In a proper world soldiers fight for the right to be free, and free thought can admit no conscription. Scotland in the 1940s did not provide a civilisation worth fighting to preserve. We were a sub-species, poor, thoughtless, dependent on the English. It was against that attitude that the fight should be.

Yet there was one factor which even in 1943 we were beginning to hear about. The name Dachau was being whispered like a dirty word, and so much underplayed was the information that the suspicion grew that Dachau was not an instrument of propaganda like the raped nuns and bayoneted babies of the first war, but a dark and terrible thing. It seemed to me that this might be that rare thing in history, a just war. Besides, I wanted to fly aeroplanes. I was still under-age but one morning I did not go into school. I went to the recruiting office and joined up. With the hindsight of nearly half a century of history I think I made the right decision.

We who live nearly at the end of the twentieth century are used to mass wickedness and mass murder. Recently a plane-load of people was murdered and fell on Lockerbie. Blood is everywhere. Yet in the 1940s, even in wartime we still believed in the basic goodness of human beings. We did not believe that gas ovens could be used on a mass scale against a civilian population. It is now clear that any country could become as wicked as Germany. Their wickedness is not personal and intrinsic to them alone. Two hundred years ago

England pursued a policy of genocide against the Scottish Highlander. Britain invented the concentration camp and used it in Africa and they also used the ancient revenge policy of indiscriminate slaughter of civilians in India and Ireland. Yet in few places have the logistics of murder been so carefully worked out as in the Third Reich. Sitting at desks with time-tables and progress sheets, civil servants did it as a matter of cold routine. That is terror at its worst. From the ghetto to the oven, the civil servants planned it all. They had their pensions to think about.

As a criminal lawyer I fight with all my ability against the power of the state. Did anyone hear a criminal lawyer speak out in Germany between 1933 and 1945? A prelate did, Pastor Niemoller, but where were the lawyers?

While I assert that what happened in Germany could happen here my instinct is different. In my youth I thought they were a better people, part of the polity of Europe, the inheritors of Greek thought, but the news of Dachau and Belsen took my innocence away. Try as I do to rejoice at the breaching of the Berlin wall, it is as though an old spectre touches my spine. When I hear Chancellor Kohl say that he has no territorial claims to make in Europe I wonder what ghost is his speech-writer. I fear the Fourth Reich.

2 The Schoolboy Goes to War

ENGLAND IS MY favourite foreign country, and my service in the Royal Air Force kept me there for nearly three years. I had expected a life where everything that moved saluted me, everything except for a few gods above me whom it would be my duty to worship. It did not turn out like that for me. Life never has. No one ever saluted me, and as for gods above I never met any. Instead I met some of the dullest and stupidest people that walk this earth. It was a fortunate time for me, although it did not seem so then. Had it been otherwise my whole life would have been different. I would have been taken into some officers mess, my father would have made me a nice smooth uniform, (he had all my measurements) and I would have been given an aeroplane to fly. If I had survived I would have returned to Scotland sanitised and civilised, a right wee anglicised Scot, all set to get on and do well. None of these thoughts was present when the schoolboy went to war.

Things went wrong almost from the start. It was 1943 and I expected to be flying within six weeks. After an interview in Glasgow and a medical and selection board in Edinburgh the Royal Air Force accepted me into the highest category of P N B. That is Pilot, Navigator, Bomb-aimer, and recommended me for a commission. There was one tough moment. At five foot six inches I was too short by an inch to be a pilot, but the doctor put his hand on my head before he measured me, and wished me luck. This should have meant certain training as a pilot. Nothing in the service is as simple as that. It takes at least two men to push a wheel-barrow and another ten to see that they do it in a smart airman-like manner. Many more must be kept in reserve in case one of the pushers contracts the Black Death or some like disease recently recognised by military medicine. They put me among the reserves.

All was going well until one of the three officers noticed that my occupation had been given as 'schoolboy'. 'Was Allan Glen's a Public School?' one of them asked. The correct answer was apparent even to a schoolboy so they got it. Yes, it was a public school. If I was there it was pretty public. After further confabulation the three officers decided that their newest recruit would be of more value to the war-effort when his education was finished. They attested me in the rank of aircraftsman second class (pilot under-training) put me on deferred service and sent me back to school. A further irony was that I was belted for truancy on my return. Thereafter, although I bombarded the Air Ministry with letters of a frustrated and often insubordinate fury, I was kept on deferred service until 1945. To be accurate there was another two week's selection board in the Summer of 1944 when I was again retained when most were not.

Many years later I read about deferred service in the history books. The Air Force fought and won an inter-service war. At the war's end they had the equivalent of two divisions on reserve, and of the best among them. They were to form a new strategic Air Force. This was a grievous loss to the other services, particularly the army. That sacred cow of Scottish military historians, the 51st Division suffered particularly, and found that they had no adequate officer corps. In Normandy they were so badly led that they failed to take their objectives round Caen, and on 15th July 1944 Montgomery considered pulling them out of the line and sending them home for retraining. Instead he replaced the divisional commander. You have to dig pretty deeply into the history books to find these facts, but the records are there.

Youngsters like myself found our period of inaction heart-breaking. We felt unworthy. There are so many choices open to the young, but mine was made, yet no call came. As a conscientious objector, my late teens would have been used in the politics of dissent inside or outside prison. Having decided to fight in the war, any other struggle had to be put aside until a later date. My life was in parentheses. An interest in the open air took me from school to a job on a farm. In these days a farm labourer spent his day working a team of Clydesdale horses and his morning and evening hand-milking his quota of eight Ayrshire cows. While I was doing this my school-fellows, who had never volunteered for anything more exciting than a rugby fifteen were being conscripted and commissioned into the local regiments and having a fine time rogering the wives and daughters of liberated Europe; or so they said. When the war ended pilots were ten a penny and flying-training was only open to officers on short term commissions. I was unwilling to be a peace-time officer, and as my deferred service did not count towards demobilisation I spent nearly three years as an A C plonk in a barrack hut. The lowest point came when, home on leave, I had to salute one of my conscripted school-fellows whom I had always despised. Mars has a sense of humour.

I stuck it and hated it to the last. We were abominably led. No officer ever spoke to me except across an orderly room table, and even then it was not on defaulters' parade. They never caught me. There were no friends to make. Everyone around me was a National Service conscript without a grain of thought or an idea that did not come from the *Daily Mirror*. Instead of friends there was, as a substitute, my love of England and the English countryside. Immediately before being called from the reserve a friend and I had rowed a dinghy from London to Oxford, sleeping in it by the way. You do not see much of the country from the surface of a canalised river but it gave me a taste of what was to come. My father, out of his great generosity and perhaps sensing my disappointment and loneliness bought me a motorcycle, a Triumph Speed Twin, one of the best and fastest of the post war generation of machines. The standard work on the English Parish Church provided me with a new interest, and I spent a great deal of time visiting them. Attendance at evensong in

21

one of the great cathedrals was magnificent theatre, but the wrong sort of audience kept trying to find a divine meaning in it. No God is as odd as his worshippers.

My interest in cathedrals led naturally to a study of the Church of England itself. The delightful dottiness of choosing its head by hereditary succession is the only fragment of the theory of the divine right of kings which has survived. Even the Church of Rome does not go that far. By comparison it is a democracy. Its head is elected, albeit on a somewhat limited suffrage. Like all old things the Church of England has taken on a lovely patina, and when they still used the Book of Common Prayer attendance at divine worship put you in the presence of poetry. A well produced Church of England service has the flavour of a Shakespearean play. There is an odd sort of reverence about this church which I can never fathom. Maybe it is patriot calling to patriot. Certainly the very Englishness of it all kept the stone of destiny quietly in my mind, not to defame a pulpit, but to advance a principle. I would show them yet.

The pulpit and the sword call all the best people, or so it is said. If this is true, the cream of them must be vicars. Maybe the military mind is the same in all countries, and has changed little through the ages. Benumbed by boredom and the dreadful solemnity of its own importance it peers at life through the wrong end of a microscope. I had a resolve to learn Latin, which I had not studied since my Paisley schooldays. This posed a problem to which the Staff College had no solution. A barrack room was not the easiest place to concentrate, as learning Latin was outwith the ken of my fellow airmen. It roused their antipathy as though it would bring down a judgment on them. Solitude for a few hours every evening in any room anywhere in the vast complex which is an Air Force Station should not have been hard to find, but it was. If the N C O's found me they ordered me away. An airman reading was an airman getting into mischief. You did not know what he was reading. I sought official help by applying to my Flight Commander for the use of an unoccupied room. The reception varied from station to station but was usually hostile. The universal service mind opens and shuts like a bi-valve and scoots out a spurt of water when faced with a new problem. Alexander got his name in the history books for cutting a knot in a piece of rope instead of untying it. His staff cheered, but any civilian would have done the same and thought nothing of it. If we civilians had not invented weapons for the military they would still be prancing about on horses and hiding in holes in the ground.

'So you want to study Latin?'

'Yes, Sir.'

'What for?'

'Some quite interesting things are written in Latin, Sir.'

That was a mistake. That was lofty insolence. Try again next time. Try the truth.

'Because I want to be a lawyer, Sir.'

'A lawyer !!! March him out, Flight Sergeant.'

Somehow the work went on and by the time I was demobilised I was reading Virgil. But I paid a price. I was shunned by my mates who to a man were from the English working class. Hardly a Scot did I meet.

The English working class are the must unassuming and unaspiring people. Servants, and the sons and daughters of a thousand years of servants they exist only to glory in their exploitation, which they get mixed up with patriotism. Their class system is so rigid as almost to be a caste system. This affects not merely the working class but all the other classes. It restricts the freedom of everyone in a way that strikes strongly at an unclass-conscious Scot. We have nothing like so much rigidity in Scotland. In education the two English Universities, of Oxford and Cambridge, have always closed their doors to anyone other than the upper classes, and until last century there was none other. There has never been the English equivalent of 'the lad o' pairts.' I read *Jude the Obscure* with astonishment. If Jude had been a Scot he would have been welcomed at any of our four universities, and not banned as an upstart. We have had and still have our depressed people in Scotland but we also have a tradition of education. From the Norman conquest to the end of the industrial revolution there were no educated working class people in England. When Neil Kinnock asked his famous question, 'Why am I the first person in my family to have had a University education?' the answer is that he was not born a Scotsman. Perhaps Karl Marx made a mis-assessment of the class system by studying it in England. If he had studied it in a country like Scotland which has never been conquered he might have found it less rigid. As an aircraftsman plonk I was very definitely of the lowest class and even the pilots I flew with did not speak to me.

This is surprising because I worked as a fitter on engines, which meant servicing aircraft for other men to fly. There is a reluctance among people who work on aircraft to fly. Perhaps they know all the things that can go wrong, and expect the wings to fall off. Pilots, on the other hand, are keen to have someone from the hangar as a hostage against careless workmanship. I thus got the chance to fly in various types of aircraft. One would have thought that there would have been a bond between me who worked on the aircraft and the officers who flew them, but this was not so. Even walking across the sacred tarmac in front of the hangar to where the aircraft was waiting for air-test the pilot walked ahead and an NCO accompanied me and strapped me in. It was the NCO who checked my harness not the pilot, as was his duty. I have since piloted aircraft for over a thousand hours, and I never opened the throttle even to taxi without personally checking that my passengers were comfortable and strapped in. It must have been some ritual of the English class system which made these young pilots behave as they did. I thought they were Gods and would have remembered anything they said to me like a treasure, but they never spoke. I enjoyed flying in military aircraft, but being treated like a sandbag made it something less than an adventure.

Adventure I found elsewhere on a parachute jumping instructor's course at Upper Heyford near Oxford. This course was for regulars only and as a volunteer on a limited engagement it was not open to me. Bluff took my way past my own C/O who was so busy discussing with his adjutant the folly of jumping in and out of aeroplanes that he did not read my documents. The adjutant was agreeing. I hoped my file might not catch up with me until the course was over. Files were always sent separately, reputedly by despatch rider, which would not surprise me. If entrusted to the Royal Mail they might fall into the hands of Russians.

The first fortnight of the course was both terrifying and exhilarating. It was probably designed to weed out those lacking the necessary keenness and it developed a competition amongst us to see who could last the course. They taught us how to fall. The concrete floors of the hangars were covered with coir mats which abraded our skin and did little to cushion us, as we were projected onto them from various heights and at various forward, backward, and sideways speeds. The apparatus was all inexpensive and had been invented and constructed by our own NCOs for whom I had a great admiration and respect. Various people fell by the wayside from various injuries, but the most common cause of failure was even a momentary hesitation to jump. Even today, if someone were to shout, 'Red light on stand in the door. Green light on. GO!'my reaction would be automatic. At the end of the first week we had to jump from a little box in the hangar roof with only an air brake to decelerate us. We wore a harness attached to a long cable wound round a drum. On the end of the drum was a small propellor which our momentum sent whirring round. In theory this was supposed to stop us breaking one or both legs. We came down with a thump, but the real test was in getting there. We had to climb an exposed vertical ladder to a height of sixty feet to get into the box. There was nothing to hold on to but the rungs and we were not harnessed up. Looking into space between one's boots made it very easy to lose focus and freeze, yet I never heard of anyone falling. It would have been fatal if he had.

That course was the only time in my service career when good leadership brought out total committment. We would not have let down those NCOs for anything. A generation earlier people like us went to their slaughter on the Somme for the same reason. It was because decent NCOs went to their death also. Look at a war memorial and you will see what I mean. Without Upper Heyford much history would be inexplicable to me. But I only lasted a fortnight.

Then came the summons to the flight office where there was a different sort of person. My documents had caught up with me and I was marched in by the discipline Flight Sergeant to meet my CO for the first time. Flanked by two flight commanders who were equal strangers to me, he looked like a male model, or an actor in brief employment. He couldn't have jumped from a bus, let alone an aircraft. He told me that it was a court-martial offence to waste the time and money of the service by coming on a regulars' only course. My plea to be allowed one drop before being ignominiously returned to unit was rejected. He was going to send me to the guard-room immediately. Probably he did not mean it, and was only trying to impress the two wingless wonders beside him, but the threat frightened me. I asked him to look at my record, and pled with him that my fault lay only, and I remember the phrase to this day, in an impatience to serve. His reaction was instantaneous. His eyes lost their focus, his eyebrows all but covered his mahogany-polished forehead, his lips parted and a surrealist fish-hook materialised at the corner of his mouth. It was the eternal soldierly look of suspicious alertness. Thus gazed the Roman soldier at the cross. I went back to my unit to the sound of my CO's oral breathing and heard no more of courts martial.

Comparing notes many years later with my friend Edgar

Prais who spent two years in the Israeli Army without being able to speak Hebrew, we found that we had had the same experiences. When asked how he had been able to serve without speaking the language, he replied bitterly, 'You must be joking. Every army uses about thirty words and you very quickly learn them.' This shows the literacy of the Jews. In the Royal Air Force they get by on twenty.

Thirty-three months in a barrack hut may have been a bitter price to pay for the boyhood ambition to go out and kill, but it taught me much. It taught me that the under-dog has feelings, however sullenly he may conceal them. Later as an aircraft owner I sought out those who worked on my aeroplane and told them how it was flying and thanked them for their services. This may have been good manners. It was also a step toward survival. My mates had looked on all pilots as bastards, and it did not make them careful workmen. Perhaps my experience helped in a wider context. In court I never make a joke at the expense of a witness or try to score any point off him, other than an evidential one. Any lay person, whether he be in the awful loneliness of the dock, or merely in the witness box is a frightened person. He is holding on to the priceless commodity of human dignity which the law exists to preserve.

The years between eighteen and twenty three are the years when a young man learns some social grace. Boyhood is behind him and he is entering on the youth of manhood. It is time for him to talk with deference to the elders of the tribe, and to court the company and society of men and women of his own age. All that passed me by. I learned to despise the elders of the tribe. I found I had nothing to share with people of my own age, yet I learned humility which may be the beginning of wisdom. And I can never look at a war grave or a war memorial without a lump in my throat and a feeling that I cheated. Most victims of war are in the eighteen to twenty-three age group and these are my wasted years. I am lucky to have survived and I owe a life to so many people of my own age who didn't.

3 Printers-ink and Poetry

THE SCHOOLROOM and the barrackroom incubated me until I was in my twenty-third year. In 1948 the eggshell broke, and I strutted out, a fluffy chick in the brave new world. It was a great place. A grateful country gave me a demob suit, a piece of paper from the King thanking me for my service, and a pamphlet telling me what to do next, which I tore up. An instruction sheet for this new thing called life was an insult. It was now my life, not theirs. My father had retired, and my mother and he had gone to live in the country, so there were no restraints. An ex-serviceman's gratuity of twelve pounds, designed to set me up for life, went on a holiday in Holland as the guest of a glorious woman, the first of many with whom I have been endlessly in love. Women are such lovely creatures. There is no compensation in age for the shy look, sparkling from under lowered eyelashes, which has not come my way for years, and to which I once so instantly responded. 'Come and take me I'll run,' it says, but they never ran fast. Fornication is fun, despite what the ministers say. Every time I see a lovely woman, I thank God for my mis-spent youth.

All the best things in life are expensive, especially lovely women, and Scottish students are poor. Enrolment at Glasgow University to study Arts and Law provided a pleasant surprise. A request to pay my fees by instalments was turned away with a smile, and I was given a copy of the pamphlet which I had thrown away. It told me how to apply for an ex-serviceman's grant. It was as though the inscrutable face of Government gave a grotesque wink. The state, having denied me the chance to fight, now lavished riches on me as though I were a hero. Not only were all fees paid, but they gave me a grant, equivalent to a labourer's annual wage. Vacation jobs earned as much again. None of it was taxed. This was wealth. These golden days gave me a standard of living to which I have ever since aspired. Ancient head-waiters still bow to me, remembering my largesse as a student. Food rationing was still in force, and the most you could spend on any one meal was five shillings. To be able to take a girl out for dinner, knowing that whatever she ate you would still be able to pay for it, was the sort of freedom from fear that wars are fought for. The lights were coming on one by one all over Europe, and I was lucky enough to be young at their illumination.

Amidst all this exuberance the light of learning did not entirely pass me by. Somewhere there are pieces of paper giving the number of subjects in which I attained proficiency. That is saying very little. An early acquaintance with classes convinced me that each professor only passed on what his own professor had taught him. Scottish history, for example consisted only of memorising great chunks of an out-of-date text book by Hume Brown. I read it for five minutes each day while sitting on the loo, memorised it, and passed without difficulty. What the professor did while committing this act of piracy on Hume Brown is not known.

No doubt the diligent student studies his subject, but the wise student studies his professor. It is like the first law of advocacy. Know your judge. The Mitchell Library is a short walk from the University, and there on shelf after shelf were the bound volumes of past exam papers. A study of them showed that any given subject came up on a three yearly rotation like turnips in a farmer's field. Spot the turnip and you were home and dry. The laziness of the professor is the saviour of the student. A few hours' work in the library was rewarded with endless time to study interesting things, or to go away and play. There is no known way to teach law. Teaching law is humbug.

A law degree is only a licence to bankrupt your client or to get him the jail. Listening to the best pleaders in court, is the only way to learn law. No one who is good at pleading is going to have time to teach. Passing examinations is all very fine, but the only subject taught at University which I found of any practical value was Logic. Without that you can't think. Many of the things memorised from books studied in my spare time have been both a delight to me and of practical use to my clients, and knowing how to use a library is a necessity. But the straight business of pleading, of persuading someone round to your client's view of things, is something which no University can teach. Flattering judge or jury into your way of thinking is of the essence of pleading, and you don't learn flattery from professors. You don't learn to say, 'My Lord is so well seized of the facts of this case that I scarcely need to mention that...' which can be the prelude to an attempt to persuade him of the well known fact that rivers run backwards to their source. I flattered my professors by memorising their pet topics and used the time saved to do a lot of living to make up for the lost years.

And living came at me with a rush and a whoosh. Then as now Glasgow University turned out great debaters, but an inherent nervousness, only conquered after many years in the courts, kept me from excelling in this fascinating art. I found instead a facility for journalism , which led me on through student newspapers into the home rule movement, and a year later into high adventure with the stone of destiny. Before that happened a lot of interesting people were to take me up, shake me up, and fill my gaping beak with worms of delight. Our first student newspaper was founded by John Weyers and myself. John Weyers later became an associate editor of *The Glasgow Herald*, although I doubt if he ever put editorship of the *Gilmourhill Girn* on his curriculum vitae. It was suppressed by the University Senate after seven issues, as they said it was suborning university discipline. Perhaps it was a success after all.

What was noteworthy about the *Gilmourhill Girn* was where it was printed. We hawked it round the smaller printing houses in the city, most of whom very wisely did not want to know us. At last we got to the Caledonian Press in Argyle Street near Anderston Cross, an area of the City since demolished. The Caledonian Press was founded and run by two brothers MacKenzie, Gaelic speakers from Lewis who had gone underground to avoid conscription. In traditional fashion, and with a fine sense of humour they had changed their name to Campbell, and some of the heat being off were on their way back from that desperate *nom-de-guerre* and had reached the half way stage of MacKenzie-Campbell. It was for the rights of people like the MacKenzie brothers that I had recently been so keen to fight. Their machinery would now be of great archaeological interest. It consisted of a Mark 1 Linotype, a great groaning flatbed, a stone, a few trays of type and a treadle platen. Both brothers were utterly and holily poor. So far as was noticeable they never paid any taxes. Probably they never earned enough. They had a genius for going unnoticed. From that little shop, with their twenty-six soldiers of lead they set out, not to make money, but to redeem their country. The great glory and bravery of it! I had found fellows at last. It was the start of a sort of unpaid apprenticeship. Only printers and advocates call their apprentices devils, and it is pleasant to have been both. For a few years I went round with printer's ink on my hands, and it has never quite gone from my blood. To this day a certain composition of the smell of burning paint and molten lead, usually from a scrap merchant's yard, takes me back in a whiff to those days at the Caledonian Press.

The Caledonian Press published many interesting pamphlets and books, none of which will be found in any copyright library. They did not believe in copyright. They believed in no right except their own. They were glorious anarchists, and disdained anything to do with officialdom. A certain amount of jobbing printing kept them in beer and fish suppers, which was all they seemed to live on. The pub next door was called the Red Lion, and they kept it rampant. They also published a newspaper called *The National Weekly*, which was owned, written, printed, and financed by themselves. Anyone can start a newspaper. Its editorial policy depended upon which brother was sitting at the Linotype when the week's editorial had to be written, and not a little on his state of sobriety at the time. After a good week's takings it could be positively benign. I cut my journalistic teeth on it with a weekly column, in return for which I was permitted to sell it on Saturday nights at the corner of Wellington Street and Sauchiehall Street, where street corner oratory was then tolerated by the police, if not admired. One, in plain clothes, was reputed to be always in attendance. The military can't have all the dunces. I tried my hand at oratory but I was no use. I got the bird. Others, like the late Oliver Brown, immediately established a rapport with the good-humoured crowd, who loved him, and would do anything in the world for him, except vote. This was a pity. His Scottish Socialist Party, which at one time consisted only of him, me and the plain-clothes policeman, would have enlivened Westminster. His cheerful irreverence, and indeed irrelevance, would have gone a long way to making Hansard readable.

Oliver Brown was not a frequent visitor to the Caledon Press, but I met another who was to have a profound influence on my life. It is a pity that so few of his contemporaries wrote about Robert Burns, and the same goes for Hugh MacDiarmid, or Christopher Murray Grieve as his real name was. Much has been written about him since, but we have to go back to his own autobiography *Lucky Poet* for anything about his early days. I knew him from 1949 until his death in the 1970s, although we lost touch in the closing years of his life. I have the Caledonian Press to thank for our first meeting.

I was setting up type by picking up each letter laboriously by hand and putting it into a 'stick' when he came in. He was a small man, with a sweep of dark hair pushed back from a high forehead. All his features were squashed down into his chin

32

and mouth leaving a small pointed nose pushing before him like a ferret's or a mole's. His voice was gravelly, and pleasantly pitched at somewhere between an enquiry and a growl. Nowadays it would be called sexy. I always picture him in a three-piece suit. Where he got it from is unknown, and not even my father could have done anything for his appearance. He did not dress. He hung clothes about him. His hands were always dirty. At first sight this appeared to be printer's ink. In *Lucky Poet* he claims that it came from thick-black tobacco which he kept loose in his pocket. Privately I think he loved Scotland so much that he preferred to carry it around on him rather than wash it off. He never obtruded. He was shy. After a few drinks a beatific smile came on his face. He tolerated and indeed loved fools. Me for a start, or at least he tolerated me. He never took a great part in any conversation but listened, and either expressed agreement, or disagreed politely. He was the master of the conversation stopper. 'The only trouble with Wendy Wood is she's a police spy,' was one of them. Sometimes I wonder if the raging C.M. Grieve I read about is the same man I knew.

Whether or not he is a major poet, rests on the judgment of my contemporaries, not on mine. They think he is great, and if we are not careful we will be having MacDiarmid Suppers, and what we would eat at them would make a good contest for one of Tom Shield's competitions in *The Glasgow Herald*. We would never have any trouble knowing what to drink. Anything, so long as there was plenty of it. Christopher Grieve would not be fussy. I doubt very much if his ghost would take kindly to that kind of worship. He used to say that only a tiny fraction of one percent of the public read any sort of poetry, and fewer still understood it. He never wrote for any sort of approbation, and that is what I found fascinating. He truly cared very much for humanity, but did not give a damn what any single member of the species thought of him or what he wrote. He would have laughed with me, when I once fell asleep during a reading of *A Drunk Man Looks at the Thistle* by Tom Fleming in the Traverse Theatre, and was asked to leave because my snores interrupted the proceedings. He preferred honest comment like that to adulation.

I never got beyond an admiration for his lyrics. Some years before we met, while searching for a copy of William Souter in a bookshop in Perth I had come across MacDiarmid's *Sangschaw*, his first volume of poems which in an unlikely fashion has a foreword by John Buchan. It was the latter's name that caught my eye. Its purchase and its contents delighted me. No one gives much thought to those early years, when he must have been assailed by loneliness. The 1920s and 1930s were grim years for Scotland, when the pulse fluttered and nearly stopped. Even the name of the country had gone. You still see its substitute on old whisky advertisements. Haig, Markinch, N B. The N B stands for North Britain. That is what they called Scotland then, but C.M. Grieve didn't. To the hoarse laughter of almost every literary figure, except John Buchan, who knew what Christopher was about and approved, C.M. Grieve set about putting our language back into print. Plastic Scots, he called it, in an infelicitous phrase. It was a lonely job. I admire him for the way he stood solid like Ailsa Craig, while the waves of contempt and indifference broke around him. He was Scotland alone then. It was a woman who sustained him, and I had the good luck to meet her too.

People who consider the lives of the poets should spare a thought for their wives. There is no contemporary paragraph on Jean Armour, and there cannot be too many on Valda Grieve, in both meanings of that expression. The poverty of going hungry, fireless, lightless, unrecognised and patronised never left a mark on her that I could see. She never went unloved. In the days long ago when I knew her she was as lovely to look at as she was by nature, with lights in her corn-coloured hair and highlights in her eyes, a Cornish pixie of a woman, a glory to know. She slipped away last year, God knows where, and I write about her here, remembering her for her warmth, not for the prickly person which other people seemed to know, for her warmth and great kindness.

I first met that kindness at their home at Dungavel. They had a cottage there from the Duke of Hamilton, and I went out to visit them. In those years at Glasgow University there was a tradition of lunch-time meetings in the Union, where speakers of various disciplines gave addresses. These were mainly political speeches, and poets were something of a novelty, but I was determined to get C.M. Grieve there. Behind that determination there was a personal and indeed secret reason. I had then decided to attempt to remove the Stone of Destiny from Westminster. Do not ask me the motive. Before that event became overlaid with publicity and hype it was a clear thing, yet intensely private. Since then it has become public, and not so clear. I quite simply wanted to make a gesture for my country, like a lover who sends flowers, however hopeless his love. This I now state. Songs and poetry had far more to do with it than reason. Homer is greater than Hercules. Songs and poetry have launched more ships than Helen of Troy. And if anyone doubts the power of a simple idea let him remember that it was one idea from one philosopher expressed in one short sentence which animated militarism, and nearly brought the world to destruction. That line is, 'The state is God walking among men'. It is an idea, good or bad, which creates events. Not money, and certainly not politicians. Whom better than a poet to discuss my idea with?

To the poet I now took my problem. I had been to Westminster Abbey a month or two before to see if it were possible. It was and I was determined to do it. Decisions taken like this are very lonely ones. I had not told a soul. There was not a soul to tell. Now I went out to Dungavel ostensibly to invite him to the Union, actually to try to find what to do next. Scotland was as lonely as that in the 1950s. There were very few of us who thought it was worth while going on. I could have discussed it with the MacKenzie brothers, but as conspirators they seemed to me to be less than type-cast. One dreary November night in 1949 I took the bus out to Dungavel.

Christopher Grieve came to the Union and delivered his speech. He was no orator and he read every word that he spoke. The meeting was a failure. Students expected Land of Hope and Glory in tartan, and when they did not get it they shouted him down. What was clear, however was that it was an essay he was holding in his hand, all written out in his crabbed writing, even to his peroration which was written in the margin, so that he had to turn the paper sideways to read it. Preparation for a fifteen minute speech had taken several days out of his life.

As for the Stone of Destiny, it was not the first time the suggestion had been made to him. Yes, it would be a wonderful thing to do. Yes, it would be an act of great symbolism, an almost poetic gesture. But as to the doing of it he was only mildly encouraging, probably because he felt that it was for a young man to decide to take his own risks. That is the sort of gentleman he was. The thought simmered with me for another year.

4 Scotland's Forgotten Patriot

SOCIALISM OR FASCISM or any of the other doctrines which will cure all the ills of mankind from poverty to the pox has never had any great attraction for me. A slow improvement in a kindly outlook towards others is all that can be hoped for. A century ago, when the Forth bridge was built there was no safety boat, and the workmen fell to their death. Nowadays, if a painter falls off, he still falls to his death. Legislation can do nothing about the force of gravity, and water is very hard when you hit it at speed. The best you can hope for is disembowelment. Nevertheless there is now always a safety boat to pick up the pieces of the painter. This compassion, however misplaced, is progress. We worry more about our fellows.

It was this attitude, not to be confused with cynicism, which kept me from joining any of the regular political parties. Membership of a political party is a sort of intellectual surrender. You affix a label to yourself, and, like your luggage on a flying holiday, you arrive at the most unusual destinations. One day you are supporting unilateral nuclear disarmament: the next day not. Inconsistency is a great virtue, provided it is your own inconsistency. My party, which no one else is permitted to join, contradicts itself daily, and is in a constant state of schism, but at least it is my own. Scotland alone mattered to me then, and it alone matters to me still. We can only act on the world through our country. Without his own community man is nothing.

It was my great good fortune to meet at this time another man after my own heart. John Macdonald MacCormick was his name, and he is Scotland's forgotten patriot. My lodgings were round the corner from where he lived, and we were soon on nodding acquaintance. He had a vivid face and perhaps I had too. He was the leader of the moderate wing of the

Scottish movement, which campaigned for some sort of ill-defined reform of our political institutions. A youngster is an extremist, so for that matter is an old man with few years left, and his moderate policies were not for me. But the Liberal Club at the University put him up as their Rectorial candidate, the Scottish Nationalists made common cause with them, and I was brought in to write the campaign literature

The Lord Rector is the titular head of Glasgow University. He is elected by the students for a period of four years. There is a tradition, amounting to a rule of conduct, that the candidate takes no direct part himself at the hustings. His letter of acceptance to his sponsors is his election address. Since we lived close to one another I fell into the habit of waiting for John MacCormick in the street, and these 'chance' meetings soon led to an invitation to his house. It became a home to me. Under his guidance the rectorial election literature took on a new direction. No doubt we were cheating, but as his ideas and mine soon became indistinquishable no one ever noticed. He taught me never to reply to any criticism, never to mention an opposing candidate by name, and above all to make everything short and readable. Rectorial elections were taken by the political parties as straws to show which way the wind would blow in the next generation. When John MacCormick won the election the Secretary of State for Scotland, a long forgotten Labour hack, said that it was of no importance, and that it had only happened because MacCormick had some of the best students on his side. I would rather be supported by some of the best students than by a bag of old bones of a Scottish Secretary.

John MacCormick would never have made a Scottish Secretary. It is not because he did not have the ability. He had that in plenty. It was because he saw clearly that you can't rule a nation with a secretary. Nor did he want to represent Scotland at the English Parliament. The only representative he wanted in England was an ambassador. 'I have not spent my life trying to be convenor of a glorified county council,' was one of his sayings. In public he advocated, 'A Scottish Parliament for Scottish affairs, an English Parliament for English affairs, and a British Parliament for British affairs.' This meaningless formula allowed us to say pretty much what we wanted without being accused of preaching treason to Westminster, which was what we were really about. The country wasn't ready yet for treason. Forty years on from John MacCormick that formula is the sort of wishy-washy nonsense that the pink tories of the Labour party now embrace. Even so they had to be levered into that position by their pals in London who fear a take over of the Labour heartland by the Scottish Nationalists.

Although he was one of the founders of the party, Scottish Nationalists were hated by John MacCormick. He had had too much of them. They are different now but in these days there was a bitterness about them that repelled. They seemed animated by hate rather than love. There was a strong racist tinge to them. Some boasted to have nothing but Scots blood in their veins, whatever that may mean. A nation composed of a mixture of Picts, Caledonians, Scots from Antrim, deserters from the Roman legions, Normans, (only a few of them, thank God) English, Flemings, Norse, Irish, Italians, Chinese, and recently Pakistanis, is a mongrel race, and has all the vigour of a mongrel. No Scot would win a prize at Crufts. Anyone is a Scot who loves Scotland, and better an Englishman than a Scot who doesn't.

During the war the Scottish Nationalist Party took an anti war stance. It was the one I had rejected as a schoolboy, but these were grown men and women. One of their leaders was Robert MacIntyre, whom I had met briefly when I had gone to their headquarters to address envelopes for them as a schoolboy. He and I each then formed an opinion of the other which has never wavered, so I had some sympathy for John MacCormick. He left the Scottish National Party over its intransigent wartime policies and founded Scottish Convention. From that grew the Scottish Covenant Association. The Covenant, a document asserting that its signatories believed that reform in the Scottish constitution was necessary was signed by over a million Scots, or so John said. I was too loyal to count them. John was before his time. We have a Scottish National Convention sitting now. What comes from it remains to be seen. Its members are not abused as MacCormick was abused. Some of it hurt, but he got used to it. He was reviled as a new immigrant, here to disrupt. Immigrant his family was but fourteen hundred years ago.

John's family came from Fionniphort in the Ross of Mull where his grandfather had been quarry-master in the quarries. Through the MacCormicks we get a glimpse of people at the dawn of written history. Adamnan's biography of Saint Columba, written in the seventh century, records that the Saint was brought from Antrim to Iona by one Cormac the Navigator. The MacCormicks of the Ross of Mull, just a stone's throw across the Sound from Iona are his descendants. John's father was a master mariner. His uncle Donald, the black sheep of the family was gatekeeper at the Western Necropolis in Glasgow where it was said that he readjusted the opening times of the cemetery gates to coincide with the closing times of the nearby pub. When not a gatekeeper he translated Shakespeare's plays into Gaelic. That is the sort of immigrant family they were.

The level-headed contemporaries of John MacCormick said he was a romantic, but behind the oratory and he was a great orator there was a deeply unhappy and concerned man. 'The pass has been sold so often, John,' I heard one say, 'that it is no use trying to guard it any more.' John smiled at such remarks and would have gone on fighting in that pass alone. He very often did. People of his own views reviled him as a trimmer. Wind and tide were against him and he could only make good his course by adjusting his sails to catch every faint breath of change. The other way was to stay rock-solid like Christopher Grieve and damn the tide. The only thing Grieve and MacCormick had in common was the end they both aimed for, and a mutual antipathy amounting to hatred. Once, many years later, I brought them together in my flat in Edinburgh. Far gone in amiability they stood together, each with his arm round the other's shoulder. 'I wonder what they'll say when we tell them about this in the morning,' said my wife. We never did. That was probably the closest they ever got.

Unlike Christopher Grieve, who looked indestructible, John MacCormick was a tired-looking man who suffered from a chronic kidney condition. He had no sales resistance. He could not kick a ball. He was the world's worst golfer. We once fought a snooker duel, and the angle was deserted after two hours with all the reds still on the table. He had no clothes sense. Once, at a jumble sale in Govan, he made a great magnanimous gesture and gave the overcoat off his back as a lesson in generosity to us all. To our mirth, and his confusion, it made half-a-crown. He was not much over five feet tall. When called upon to address an audience he looked at them in silence until the air fairly tingled with his personal magnetism. It wasn't a gimmick. He was wondering what to say. Then he delivered with the utmost clarity in rising quarters and descending thirds, a discourse which had even the most cynical audience oohing and aahing. He made pygmies feel giants. He made Scots feel great. His speeches were unquotable, immemorable and ephemeral, yet no one who heard him ever forgot him. Few supported him, except his family.

His wife Margaret had to put up with his long absences. John was married to Scotland. There was no glory in it for her, but she too was a devoted Scotswoman, and certainly not one to look for reward other than that provided by keeping his home and their family together. She put up with all John's absences and perhaps even more difficult, she put up with the long night sessions, when John and I talked Scottish history and Scottish constitutional law. They lived up a close which was still lit by gas. The lamplighter came round night and morning with an acetylene flame on a long pole to light and extinguish the lamps, and the clatter of his equipment on the close wall when morning came was our signal to call it another day. Dawn is the time for a young man to go to bed. John was no longer young, and he poured himself out for me as though he were an endless wine.

At these meetings and discussions I learned just how fragile the Scottish cause had become. The early Scottish home rule movement existed on faith, hope, and chicanery. Since the will was paralysed it was necessary to convince the patient that he was in the best of health. There was no television and they would not have us on the wireless. We had the greatest difficulty getting any press coverage, except in the local newspapers. There was no money and hidden from all the members was an enormous overdraft guaranteed by John and his great friend Bertie Grey. They were always on the verge of personal bankruptcy, as the terrified bank manager was always threatening to call in the overdraft. Always it edged up instead of down. From about 1928 until the coming of television John travelled Scotland and spoke in every city, town, and village. For five years I stumped the same circuit. Public meetings are now out of fashion, but in those days John, or latterly myself with perhaps another for company would get to the town somehow and address a gathering of anything from ten to a couple of hundred people.

It was preaching to the converted and the only hecklers were the Scottish Nationalists who regarded disrupting our meetings as sport. Their opposition exhilarated me. Moderation in all things was the mask from behind which we spoke, and it certainly fooled the nationalists, although I suspect they disliked me personally. I lived a far from unostentatious social life and these fundamentalists had a whiff of the Ayatollah about them. I could not resist poking fun at their awful solemnity. Scottish Nationalists seem to have changed of recent years. Maybe the old school has died out. I met one of them recently. Aged about eighty he was off to England with Scots pound notes, hoping to be insulted.

Anything I know of public speaking I learned from John MacCormick. He taught me to abhor microphones. The best amplifier is a cathedral. The experience of pitching my voice to the back of the largest hall taught me how to be heard even in the back row of the public benches of a large court-room. If the public come to hear justice administered, they should not have to strain to listen. Half the misreporting of cases in the press is because some advocate or some judge does not know his job, and the poor reporter only hears mutter mutter mutter. I never wrote out my speeches and I still don't. A written speech is fit only to be passed round for silent reading. Only ministers of God and ministers of Government read speeches. Listen to one, if you can bear to, and you will see what I mean.

After the speeches we left behind us an embryo organisation. This might be one name on a piece of paper, or a good-going social and semi-political party like the Inverness Branch of the 1950s. The trouble was that we could give them no work to do. Keen supporters ask, 'Now that I'm converted, what do I do next?' To that question we had no answer. What we really wanted them to do was to infiltrate the two major political parties and be a fifth column. However having spent an evening attacking the parties, it was far too Machiavellian to say to our converts, now go and join a political party and convert it to our way of thinking. Besides, they might have been reconverted. Political parties can fight elections, throw up charismatic and ambitious figures, and give a sense of victory and personal fulfillment both to the principals and to the supporting cast. We could not do that. If we were to go to the hustings we would have been annihilated. We had to pretend that the principles of the Scottish Covenant were so fundamentally imbued in every Scottish voter that they transcended all political beliefs and narrow partisan issues of creed or politics. This was humbug. The truth was that the Scots had still not regained sufficient self-confidence to want to govern themselves and we knew it. We tried to keep the light alive, waiting for daybreak, but it was often a heart-breaking task.

Sometimes I wonder if the dawn has really come. Just a few weeks ago I was speaking to a successful young businessman who by his own energies has pulled himself up to have a substantial transport enterprise. He is a devout Tory. There is nothing wrong with that, although my views are different. What astounded me was that he didn't think Scotland could quite manage her own affairs. If I had suggested that his business should be put into the same tutelage as his country he would have thought I was mad.

If the Scottish Covenant Association was ever hampered by any sort of written constitution no one ever knew what it was. Like the British Constitution it was elastic, *a priori*, capable of infinite adjustment to meet any situation, yet quite incapable of any formal amendment without the whole fabric falling into a heap of dust, as it ultimately did when John MacCormick sickened and died. It had a National Council on which were various lay, ecclesiastic and minor political figures. Membership of it qualified you for never being in the Honours List and for nothing else. You never got invited to the Queen's garden party either. The National Council only met when it was summoned by John, rather like the Estates General of France. Again like the Estates General the usual cause for its meeting was that the Association was broke again, and John wanted the luminaries to put their names to a 'National Appeal'.

All this time, while carrying the Covenant's overdraft, John was trying to earn a living as a solicitor, and bringing up a young family. His faith moved me, and I am nearly a mountain where faith is concerned. When the National Council met, John was in for a grilling until the time came for the members to catch their last tram home. John wore them down until they voted with him, usually *nem con*. It was a hobby, a mere thing apart to the Members of Council; it was life itself to John MacCormick.

One member of the National Council sticks in my mind above all others. He was the Very Reverend Doctor Neville Davidson, minister of Glasgow Cathedral. He was a good man according to his lights, and had lived a good life, had never done anything wrong, had never done anything at all in fact. As minister of one of our great ecclesiastical charges he could always command a paragraph or two in the newspapers, so he had to be placated. In its members' view the National Council met to formulate policy. In John's view it met to put its name to a fund-raising appeal, and in this divine's view it met so that he could call John to account for some minor change of policy which John, to suit some whiff of public opinion, had just made. The divine sat unmoved, his lips closed in awful disapproval, his whole demeanour regardant of a new sin beyond the contemplation of the decalogue, until John's eloquence or chicanery or the imminence of the last tram home won him round. But worse; he would then take up John's position, immovable as a rock, long after John had passed to some new and often contradictory view into which the divine had again to be levered. They were both so solemn about it that they made a better comic turn than a God-Slot like Late Call.

If the Covenant was a one-man ship it was on the right course. For two decades in the 1940s and 1950s it kept Scotland alive and ever before a public who shied away from 'narrow nationalism', as anything more rational was called. The electorate voted with equanimity to be governed by their hereditary enemies in the south-east corner of this island, and complained illogically at the result, but they listened to John

45

MacCormick. Sea changes do not come to a country overnight. They have to be worked for. John won over the Liberal Party to his policies and the Labour Party has now followed. It is as though my old horse Rosinante has been saddled by Donald Dewar. I rode her to death when I was a young romantic and he is welcome to her, but I am afraid she will not take him far. Socialists have always been quite good Scots when out of office. When in Government they have never delivered, nor will they ever deliver. Any significant devolution must be at the expense of Scots representation at Westminster, and that would mean the death of Labour as an alternative party of English government. Labour requires the Scottish contingent of lobby fodder to give it a majority. As he and Rosinante plod along I wonder if Donald's conscience troubles him. Sometimes there is a change in him. He may yet become a convert to the views he so eloquently expresses. Make no mistake, behind that honest facade there is a very cunning man. He knows as well as we do that he is the Uncle Tom of Scotland. He is here to see that we cotton-pickers in the North do nothing to annoy the London plantation owners and their Southern belles. If we do, they might not vote for his party, and where would he be then? The North Face of Donald Dewar is as yet unclimbed.

Lest I be thought to be a Tory let me say that I regard the Scottish Conservative Party as a twentieth-century joke. Its few remaining members of Parliament have been stranded by the tide and lie on the beach like woebegone porpoises. No self-respecting Scot could give his life to such a party unless his ambition outruns his patriotism. But the philosophy is still alive, and when Scottish conservatism shakes off its London puppet-masters it will have something valuable to give. It may yet revive and be an important force, but I do not see that happening until self-respecting Scots can join it without being laughed at. I have a spy in the Appin Tories whose name I would not reveal for a kingdom. At a meeting not so long ago they were discussing whom they could approach to be their titular chairperson. One name was mentioned, and after a pause someone voiced the feeling of the meeting. 'We can't have him,' said the voice. 'He's got a Scots accent.'

John MacDonald MacCormick had a Scots accent and he wore himself out in the service of the Scots. If there is a Valhalla for selfless persons he will be drinking in it. He won't be in heaven. He was aye against heaven. If he ever got there he would long since have been thrown out for annoying the neighbours and suborning God to give a fair crack of the whip to ordinary people. He died of a broken heart because he thought he had failed. He left a whole people as his monument.

5 The Stone of Destiny

FOR A WHILE I was a pessimist about Scotland. I thought it might end, although never in the tartan Ruritania my friend Sir Nicholas Fairbairn fears more than the resident reds under the beds of Fordell Castle. It won't. Yet England will not keep faith for all that is done and said. She will not willingly hive off her most ancient and richest province, but once the Scots unite, as they are doing now, it does not matter what England thinks. Despair has always been our worst enemy. Despair has gone and our country's heart is sound. But its heart is not at Westminster.

How Westminster Abbey first came into my mind is a curious story. Take away a country's history, and the country withers. England is not daft, and every time the English invaded they took whatever historical records they could find. In the 1930s, under pressure from Scottish historians, England returned some of the medieval Exchequer Rolls. The Scottish press was then universally hostile to Scottish aspirations but there was one exception. *The Bulletin*, the sister paper to the *Glasgow Herald* was edited by J.M. Reid who was a nationalist mole, and who wrote nationalist pamphlets under the *nom-de-plume* of Colin Walkinshaw. When the Exchequer Rolls arrived in Edinburgh Wendy Wood, God bless her, paraded along the Royal Mile bearing a placard inscribed, 'England disgorges some of the loot, but where is the Stone of Destiny?' A picture of this was published in the *Bulletin*, and I saw it as a small boy, just newly and proudly able to read.

My mother read the *Bulletin*, and when asked about this picture she told me about the Stone of Destiny. She told me how it had been brought to Iona along with the first Scots settlers, long ago, and how ever since it had been the symbol of the Scottish people. She told me that we did not need silver or gold or banners and flags to show that we were a people,

48

and that this rude block of stone had always been enough. All the Scottish kings had been crowned on it. 'And there have been among us one hundred and ten kings and not one foreign-born among them,' she said, not knowing that she was quoting directly and accurately from The Declaration of Arbroath. Why was it in England?' asked the little boy, and she told me that it was a long sad story. That Edward I of England, the Hammer of the Scots had invaded Scotland and taken it away, and although, thanks to Wallace and Bruce the English had been driven out, the Stone had never been returned. She left it at that, and I put aside the *Bulletin*, wondering. People who parade the streets with placards, and newspaper editors, who have to hide their true opinions should never say die. Children may be watching and paying heed.

The childhood memory was recalled for John MacCormick. He was the ideal man. In wartime, my ambition to fly a fighter aircraft, the most personal and comfortable way to kill a fellow human, had come to naught, and no explanation had been given to me as to why I was not wanted. Instead, circumstances had forced me to cultivate loneliness, a habit which has ever continued with me, but with John MacCormick I was in total communion. At twenty-five a young man soars and gallops, everything to be done is done instantly and at the high lope. The stone could have been done like that, but it wasn't. We stood back for a while and took a long look at it.

The long look took me to Westminster Abbey again. This was not just a reconnaissance to see if it was possible. This was with full intent. In those days Westminster Abbey was a gentlefolk's church, not a Disneyland. I joined the respectful visitors and moved round with them until we came to the Chapel of Edward the Confessor where the coronation chair sits. It is reputed to be the oldest piece of furniture still used for the purpose for which it was made. That purpose was to contain the Stone of Destiny. It is a high-backed chair, made of oak, and underneath the seat is a shelf which contains the stone. Every English sovereign since 1306 has been crowned on it. It should have been daunting, but it wasn't. It was high adventure. Closer examination showed that there was an oaken cornice round the stone, which would have to be jemmied away, but after that the stone would slip out easily. Well, comparatively easily.

It was a great rough piece of sandstone, as big as a sack of coal, and it weighed more than four hundredweight. The route from the Edward Chapel was a poser. The way in was up a few wooden steps and manhandling such a weight down these steps would be awkward. The other way was through into the nave past the high altar. I did not dare to try the doors to the high altar to see if they were kept locked. This would have drawn attention and they would have put me out with shame and contumely. High altars are not for tourists. All was done with reverent circumspection. Circumspection is all right but I had to take a risk with the door from the outside of the Abbey into Poets' Corner. A good kick and a shove when no one was looking showed that it could be jemmied open from the inside, and outside there was a lane with no apparent barrier to stop a car being backed up to the door. That part seemed simple.

What was not so simple was recruiting the team. John MacCormick and I talked about it at length. Three seemed the ideal number. The more people who knew the more chance there would be of someone talking. Recently John had introduced me to Kay Mathieson, who was a keen worker for the Covenant Association. She came from a Gaelic-speaking family in Wester Ross, and was a domestic science student. Her father, a master mariner, had been lost at sea when his ship had been torpedoed under him. The Gaelic language, and the people who speak it have been the prime interest in her life, and she still teaches Gaelic in Wester Ross. In these days she was small and dark and remote as a Hebridean Island, a bonnie bonnie young woman, yet it is her concentrated degree of remoteness that is most memorable. Of all the people I have met and worked with she is the one I got to know least. This is a pity, and my great loss, as there was much to know. Kay could drive a car, which not many of us could do in those days. My wartime driving licence covered all vehicles, but I had to teach myself the business of driving on the way to London. There was no time for lessons.

Ideally two cars are needed for this sort of enterprise. One to do the job, and one to make off with the loot. That is what my clients do, and we did the same. One was hired, and the other was provided by Alan Stewart, a fellow student. He volunteered at the last moment to join his friend Gavin Vernon who was our number three. Number four was a supernumerary. He was never a supercargo. Without him we would have failed. Both cars were Ford Anglias of considerable vintage. Five years after the war's end new cars were a rarity. In these two cars the four of us set off on a bleak December day in 1950, down the black narrow road to London, to hurt no one, except England's vanity, to save no one except the ruined hopes of our own country.

It was all as casual as that. We had no money for hotels, and barely enough for food and petrol. Indeed we ran out of our meagre supply of money, and at one point had to phone home and beg some more. Looking back after forty years the naivety of it takes my breath away, although the young will not think it is naive. Truly we did not know the size of what we were taking on. None of us thought that it would still be talked of forty years later, and it is still with a sort of astonishment that I realise that it is. Since then I have made friends with people who have fought in great battles. Their attitude is sometimes, Yes, it was a rare tear. More often they say that it was just a case of keeping your head down, and plugging on. I second that latter attitude. I may be a poor second, but I know what they mean. To the fury of people who were not there and want to know more, you can't tell what it was like, because you just got on with it, recording few emotions, and scarcely ever articulating your thoughts.

A Touch of Treason

Of course we knew that we would go to jail, but that was never discussed. We accepted the risk without thought, and if there was any personal hope it was that the sentence would not be a long one. We feared ridicule more than jail, and if we had failed we would have been ridiculed to this day. The fickle public is as quick to jeer as to cheer. The public aspect of what we did concerned us very little if at all, and certainly not until much later. For my part at least I had to invent the motive later. Such inventions are necessary to try to to explain a private act to a curious public, to put words to thoughts that were never at the time expressed, and probably were not even formulated.

In its whole essence this was a private act of four young people. That cannot be stressed too highly. To me, who can now speak so glibly in Court for other people, the task of explaining what we thought is almost insurmountable. We never sang *Scots Whae Hae*. *Flower of Scotland* was not written then, and if it had been, I do not think any one of us would have known the words. I still don't. A resolution, amounting very nearly to the tearfulness of despair, was what animated me. I cannot speak for the others. We were very young. We were very ordinary people. We yearned, and yet like almost all young people we were inarticulate. We just felt that something had to be done for our country, or we would burst. It is so easy to pose. In later years the temptation to talk of saving the soul of our country, of giving back its identity to our nation, was thrust upon us by others. Since there is a murder in the cathedral of everyone's life I am willing to go along with all these high flying ideas, but to be honest the actuality was different. It was naivety as much as faith that took us down that road to London. Perhaps it is because we had faith that we built better than we knew. All these years later, I who have no faith and who am dry and tearless weep with pride for the faith of these four young people one of whom was once myself. It was a grimness that took us past Glasgow Cross and along London Road, a grimness and a faith.

We complain about the roads today, but in those days the London road had changed little since the day of the stage coach. It had been tar-macadamed and that was all. In its four hundred mile length there was not a mile of dual carriageway. The hedges were only a ditch-width away, and the on-coming headlights came straight at you at forty miles an hour. Fast, that was. Overtaking took a long time. A Ford flat out did hell-for-leather at fifty-five, wandering a bit on the outside lane. There were few cars in those days. Wise people travelled by train but you could not bring the Stone of Destiny back by train. It took us eighteen hours to reach London, alight with Christmas decorations. My English friends maintain it was a dirty Scotch trick to come down on them at Christmas, an English festival, but not then a Scots one. Truly our deed needed darkness and the Christmas holiday was the only time we would not be missed from our usual haunts.

The plan called for darkness not only to conceal our activities outside the Abbey, but to conceal me in a hiding place inside. A jemmy hung from a sling beneath my coat, and various other housebreaking tools were stowed in my pockets. The Poets' Corner door was to be jemmied open from the inside at midnight, and the other three would then enter and help me to carry out the enterprise. It did not go like that. Soon the Abbey was deserted and I lay down in a nook behind a statue, so prone and still that a line of saliva dribbled wetly and unstoppably from my mouth on to my arm. The lights went out and a grateful darkness surrounded me. My hiding-place would have been perfectly safe, but a more remote part where some war damage was being repaired seemed safer. A half an hour passed and I was creeping my way to this sanctuary, my shoes in my hand for the sake of silence, when a torch light came round the corner and the night-watchman confronted me.

'I'm locked in,' I said. A statement of the truth is the most disarming gambit.

A Touch of Treason

He looked at me for what seemed ages, and I sensed he was as surprised and afraid as I was. We stood united in the pool of light from his torch, with the great soaring darkness of the Abbey around us. This seemed to be the end, a fatal fall right at the start. But he was a kindly man. Seeing he was in no danger he relaxed, and asked me for my name and address. I replied with a false and humble agility. Sensing there was something wrong in my manner he asked if I was homeless, and offered me money before he bade me put my shoes on and turned me out the west door. That man taught me a lesson in humility which I have never forgotten. It was the first time I met charity in a Christian church.

This early set-back did nothing to dismay us. We had been caught but we were still the same people we had been an hour before, and we had learned much. That the Abbey was deserted at night seemed a certainty. One night-watchman was all there was, and I had once been a nightwatchman. A fire and a good book pass a nightwatchman's hours away, and unless we beat drums and played the bagpipes, it was unlikely that we would bring him down on us. If we could not break out from the inside, we would have to break in from the outside. Further reconnaissance was needed.

In these days the streets round Westminster were deserted. I do not know what they are like now, but we made our reconnaissance without let or hindrance. From the door to Westminster Hall, in which William Wallace faced his accusers, and through which I was later to enter to plead cases in the House of Lords, a long view could be taken of the south east aspect of the Abbey including Poets' Corner door, which had long seemed the most vulnerable entrance. A lane led up to the door, and between the Abbey and the lane, over against the flying buttresses, a line of builder's scaffolding hid a builder's yard where masons kept their materials for repair of the war-damaged fabric of the building. This yard was not secured, and it offered good cover. If we could force the door to Poets' Corner, we could take the Stone into the yard. A small car backed up the lane would not be conspicuous from the roadway, and the stone could be loaded from the yard, without too much fuss and danger. So it seemed to us, and there was no reason to suppose the Abbey watch was disquieted by our earlier misadventure.

We waited two days to let things quieten down, and that took us to Christmas Eve. On Christmas Eve we parked one of the cars on a bombed site, and backed the other up the lane to the unlocked door of the builder's yard, adjacent to the door of Poets' Corner, where we left Kay sitting in it as the driver. I wonder what she was thinking as she watched the three of us taking the jemmy to the door. I never never knew.

Jemmying a door is not as easy as it sounds. When the crack opens and the first splinter falls you glance round in fear, showing the white of an eye. From then on all is lawlessness. You are committed. Talking won't get you out of it. The door opened with a great splintering creak, and we were into the Abbey. The dim light at the far end of the nave left the rest of the Abbey in a foggy darkness. We swept along the Poets' Corner and up into the Edward Chapel, past the tomb of Edward I, Hammer of the Scots, whose dead bones Bruce feared more than any living ones, the same Edward who had removed the Stone from Scotland and whose action we were there to redress. In these short instants I was more alive than I had ever been before. There was no time for fear. The barrier before the throne was pulled back in an instant, and I jemmied away the wood holding the Stone in its place. The three of us heaved at the Stone, tugging and pulling, getting in each other's way. It came out with a thump on to the floor, and broke into two pieces, one bit being a quarter of the whole. It was a good thing it broke. As later events were to show, I had to heft the whole stone into the car by myself, and I doubt if I would have managed it in its entirety.

I betray myself. So often have I been asked about that

moment, and how I felt, that over the years I have put on an act of sacrilegious horror, and pretended shock. Having laid our sacrilegious hands on the Coronation Stone, upon which royal sovereigns are crowned, *we broke the thing*, and in a not so distant age would have been broken on the wheel. We should at least have had the decency to be horrified. Even self-preservation might have instructed such a feeling. A command to put that back just as you found it, could not now be obeyed, even if we had had any thought of obeying it. We had no such thought. Nor did we think then, although the thought is with me now, that the very moving of the Stone from its ancient seat constituted more than a touch of treason. It is a touch which has ever continued with me. My reaction is truly narrated above. It was one of relief. It would make the job of handling it easier. Everything at a time like that is done in an instant, and in a rush. Contemplation and attitudinising come later.

I whipped off my coat and laid it on the chapel floor. We put the larger bit of the stone on the coat and dragged it through the doors to the area beside the high altar, the doors I had thought might be kept locked. Then we bumped it down the steps to the nave. It was heavy, and the three of us could not have carried it between us. I picked up the broken quarter, which weighed about a hundredweight and ran with it to the car. Kay was there and wordlessly she opened the boot. The boot closed on it, and Kay got into the driving seat. To my surprise she started the engine, and I realised it must be a signal. I glanced up and saw a policeman's helmet glimmering in the wan gaslight that briefly lit the lane. I got into the car and swiftly got into a clinch with Kay. It was our only defence.

There was something human about the bobby-on-the-beat. Cars may be efficient, but they dehumanise. This was a nice young policeman. If he were still in the force he could give lessons in politeness to so many who bully around the streets in modern times. He asked us what we were doing and I told him a monstrous lie about being too late to go to a hotel, and we sat and held hands before him. Poor fellow. He offered his cigarettes to us and we smoked with him, and chatted. As we chatted I heard a rumble and thump from behind the builder's scaffold. So did he. It was the other two manhandling the large part of the stone down as arranged. The policeman stiffened. I gave a great cough and laugh and the noise stopped. The policeman slowly relaxed, and with a remark that we should be on our way, and that it being Christmas Eve not a policeman in London would want the trouble of running us in, he bade us farewell. We drove off, leaving him standing watching us. Poor, poor fellow. I record that he did not suffer over much for his humanity. Later, requests were made, by me among others, that he be not punished, and he was not. Us thieves have our honour.

Kay and I drove God knows where, and she set off alone with her part of the stone. I found my way back to the Abbey and went in again. All was silent and darkness. I had left my torch, I forget where. Only the dim light burned at a lofty mile's distance at the west door, as it had always burned. In the medieval gloom I retraced all our steps. Back to the throne, down past the altar, round the back into the Edward Chapel, groping my way, and then back to the Poets' Corner door. Nothing. Then I went into the builder's yard and found the other part of the stone. Of the other two not a sign.

I broke into a run to where we had left the other car, and careless of discovery ran through the empty streets. The car was there, abandoned. It looked very much like failure, and in the sweaty darkness I was alone, frightened and friendless. I had not even the keys of the car. I broke into a run back the way I had come. If the car was still there the other two did not have the keys of the car either. They had been in my coat pocket, and if they had not found them, they must have fallen from my pocket as we dragged the Stone along on my coat. I went into the Abbey for the third time that night and began to crawl on my hands and knees all along the way we had come, feeling with my hands before me. Nothing. Then in desperation I struck matches, whose brief light did nothing at all to illuminate the vast darkness. As despair came over me I put my foot on something, and went racing back to the car. I had found the keys.

I got the car and backed it up the lane again. That was the fourth time that lane had seen me that night. The police seemed to be blinkered, and not one did I see. I parked the car beside the scaffolding where the three hundredweight or so of the Stone was lying and wondered what to do. There was only one thing to be done, and with a great heave and a crunch that brought the old Ford's springs down on to their bearers, the Stone was in the back of the car and I was driving away. I cared not where I went and I sang as I drove. Mindless singing, triumphing in an ambition fulfilled. Implications would come later. We had been lucky, but we had pressed on regardless, and been regardlessly rewarded.

For our chance separation we had made no rendezvous. The other two, seeing us drive off, and not finding the car keys, had thought that all was lost but it wasn't. By luck, in a street not far from the Abbey, I came upon them, walking disconsolately away. The car, already lopsided on its springs from the weight of the Stone was clearly no vehicle to carry three people as well, so only one of my two companions joined me. We pooled our money, leaving Gavin to telephone home for his train fare, and Alan and I drove away and left him. It was now only a two-man job.

We were still adrenalised and we needed it because we were short of sleep. It was now broad daylight, and after the night's shenanigans we felt as conspicuous as a circus come to town. The first thing was to hide the Stone. This was not easy. Then as now South-East England was all conurbations and suburbia. Our journeyings took us as far west as Malbourough and as far south as Rochester. First we left the Stone wide open in a field, sure that we would be arrested that morning, and certain that we could pass word to someone else to finish what we had started. Would not the police be stopping every Ford Anglia? Remember, in those days the roads were empty. There were grown men and women who had never seen the inside of a car. Cars were not, as they now are, almost everyone's curse. But as the day went on and no police car stopped us, we realised that our reasonable apprehension was misplaced. We returned, retrieved the Stone from its open hiding place and hid it in a wood beside the main road north from Rochester in Kent. It was not until we were well on our way home that we were stopped by a grumpy police patrol, breathing beer and turkey for it was still Christmas Day. We bluffed our way through.

Our arrival in Scotland astonished us. I had telephoned my friend Bill Craig who was privy to the plot, but who had been unable to come with us. He had told us that, everyone was talking about it. That we had been on the news. That it was the talk of the town. Nothing prepared us for the sensation when the newspapers came out. In these days Scottish newspapers published on both Christmas Day and Boxing Day. Since their English colleagues were on holiday there was only Scottish news for them to publish. Nothing was coming over the wires. But when the English newspapers resumed publication everything else, and I mean everything else, was banished from the front pages. Scotland had become news. I remember thinking, because I had authorial ambitions, that maybe someday I could write a pamphlet about it.

Our adventures did not end with our return to Scotland. It was not enough to leave the Stone in an English wood, under an unofficial English hedge. We had to go back down to get it. Two weeks later, accompanied by Bill Craig, and yet another friend, Johnny Jocelyn, I again took the road south. This time, such is the fragrance of success, we had managed to borrow a powerful car. It even had a heater.

If our adventures on Christmas Eve and the early hours of Christmas morning were unusual enough, the finale was plain picturesque. A road ran beside the trees where the Stone was hidden, and between the road and the trees was a grassy balk, about fifty feet across. It was dark when we reached it, and as we passed we saw three or four gypsy caravans and some horses tethered nearby. We turned at Rochester and set the milometer on the car to register the correct spot. When we returned we discovered that the gypsies were stationed like a guard on the Stone. It was clear they would not move that night, and indeed they might be in semi-permanent encampment.

I had read George Borrow, and this new fact was as strange as anything in *Lavengro* or the *Romany Rye*. More practically, we knew that gypsies were a people apart, living their own lives, and such people are harassed by the police. The police of any age have no time for eccentrics. There was no basic assumption that gypsies would be on the side of what Mrs Thatcher now loves to call Law and Order. We parked the car a hundred yards away and walked down to the fire.

An ancient gypsy couple sprawled against the fence, their feet outstretched to the blaze. Beyond the circle of firelight the night was a rimey dark. Only an occasional car passed along the road. We sat down beside them in silence. They glanced at us but said nothing. At length one of my two companions, Bill Craig started to speak. He explained that we came from a small northern country many hundreds of miles away, where the gypsies were our own people. He spoke of Johnny Faa and Kirkletham, and of the broken clans, of the MacDonalds and the MacFees and the Townshends, and of the country that had never pestered or persecuted any travelling people, whatever their race. The couple listened in silence, perhaps understanding nothing, except the sincerity in his voice.

'We need something out of that wood,' said Bill. 'It's illegal, but it's not wrong. 'There was a long silence. A branch fell from the fire sending a shower of sparks into the dark lift, and the man gypsy pushed forward his booted foot and shoved it back into the embers.

'You can't get it just now,' he said. 'There's a stranger at the next fire.'

We sat through a long silence, staring at the fire as though it contained all wisdom and all knowledge. Then a man rose from a fire some distance away, got on to a bicycle, and rode away.

'You can get it now,' said the gypsy as though it were the most natural thing in the world.

We brought the car down and put the Stone in it, and I returned, near to tears to thank them. They just watched the fire and we drove away. In all the wild talk and press publicity they never breathed a word. The simplicity of humble people is the finest thing in the world.

And that is how we brought the Stone of Destiny back to Scotland. We brought it across the border on a side road over the river Esk between Langton and Canonbie. Writing these words forty years later brings back the enormous satisfaction we all felt. It has never left me.

We woke Scotland. The newspapers of that period wrote of little else, Scottish and English alike. Rewards were offered by the press, and withdrawn when the public refused to buy newspapers which tried to sell themselves by selling us. One policeman summed up the Scottish attitude when he went on record as saying, 'Aye we're looking for them, but no' so damned hard that we'll catch them.' Meantime the Stone lay hidden.

The police interviewed me almost immediately, and I managed to talk my way out of suspicion. The weeks went on and it was obvious that the net was closing. In March I was again interviewed by a posse of police, consisting of a Detective Superintendent and a Chief Inspector from Scotland Yard, and what seemed to be the entire Scottish Special

Branch, as they were then called. I kept my cards to my chest, and made no admissions, but it was clear that they had enough evidence to prosecute. They left me to sweat in a room, told me it would be 'better for me to come clean', and then questioned me at length. The Scottish police were charming and amused. The two Englishmen,(one of whom was Irish) were not so charming, and not at all amused. Later I was to cross-examine almost every one of the Special Branch in my avocation of advocate. A rapport was formed that morning that went on for years. Going through the mill taught me much. Not a few acquittals for future clients were earned and learned that morning. Then they set me free. Still the Stone was world news. Stealing a hunk of sandstone, for God's sake. It charmed everyone from Tokyo to Timbuktu. But not the English establishment.

What to do with the Stone was the problem. All sorts of negotiations went on. Predictably the Church of Scotland would have nothing to do with it. They had their invitations to the royal garden party to think of, and the Royals were said to be very vexed. Every Scot wanted it to stay in Scotland. No one in power would stand up and say so. I wanted to champ a bit off it every week and send it to London for analysis, just to keep them from sleeping too soundly, but of course I was wrong. You can't champ up your country's symbol.

Having set the heather alight our only job was to lie quiet. It was suggested to me that I should run away abroad to avoid a prison sentence. That was not the way I saw it at all. Speculation had abounded as to who were the culprits, perpetrators, or heroes, depending on your viewpoint. After the police questioned us, when all hung fire, it was known who was responsible. The press in this country could not publish for fear of contempt proceedings, should prosecution follow, as was expected. There was a waiting hush. During all this time life had to be lived. We went about the daily process of living, and let life flow over us. I do not remember being afraid, although I remember very much wondering how it would all end.

No deals were done. And still the problem persisted. It was growing a bit stale. The public wanted something to happen. My view was we should continue to lie doggo. I was wrong again. If the Stone of Destiny was Scotland's great totem, it could not be hidden for ever. It had to be produced. Two things could happen then. It could be whipped south immediately, or England could bend in moderation, and let it stay. False hope. England never bends in moderation, particularly after the lion's tail has been twisted until it comes out by the roots. They were laughed at by the world, and laughter is a more potent weapon than armies. But the problem went on.

We solved it in as moderate a way as we had created it, and with an eye to history. In 1320 after the Scottish wars had been fought and won, the Community of Scotland met at Arbroath, and in the Great Declaration warned Robert Bruce that he was a constitutional king, 'but if he should in any way betray us to the English we shall cast him out and elect another from amongst us...for it is not for glory, not for honours, not for riches that we fight but only and alone for freedom, which no good man gives up but with life itself.' On 11 April 1951 we laid the Stone of Destiny, now repaired and in its entirety, on the ruined high altar of Arbroath Abbey. It was whipped south immediately. No prosecution followed. The people of Scotland judged us, and the Home Secretary intimated in the House of Commons that the 'thieves and vulgar vandals' were known, but it would not be in the public interest to prosecute. 'Thieves and vulgar vandals', has since aye been one of my favourite phrases.

The incident is remembered to this day, not without controversy. Predictably the old guard of the Scottish Nationalists see us only as betrayers, who returned the Stone, not us youngsters who risked our liberty in taking it.

A Touch of Treason

Counterfeit stones have turned up. One is in the People's Palace on Glasgow Green. This is a good thing. Had the real Stone been left in Scotland in 1951, it would have gone to the crown room in Edinburgh Castle, and been forgotten. What Scot goes to see the Scottish regalia there, the oldest in the world, with all its fabulous history? Scots remember the Stone of Destiny because we are a thrawn people, and we love to have a grudge against the English. They are not all that idle in giving us one.

But is it the real Stone? The Stone we took from Westminster is the one we returned. I give my personal guarantee on that. But was it the real stone? There is still a mystery. That stone does not fit the ancient description. There is a lot of red sandstone around Scone from where Edward stole it, and he may have been palmed off with a counterfeit. If so why was it not produced when Bruce, ever a stickler for tradition, particularly where his Gaelic people were concerned, had secured our country? To that mystery I can give no answers. The Knights Templar may know the answer. I am not one of them.

I won fame and fortune with the Stone of Destiny. The fortune came from writing the story, as I have told it here, and selling it to the *Sunday Express*. I never touched a penny. It went to pay off the Covenant overdraft, and to finance several years of further campaigning for self-government. Fame is the spur for many people but having experienced it, it is not for me. It invades your privacy. People stop you in the street. They stare at you. For a while it was invigorating to speak at meetings where the hall was packed and the audience cheered. But that soon palled. The other side of the coin is that you are expected to be a one-subject man, ever ready to talk on your subject, a raree-show to be pointed out, an instant lecturer to be switched on by any stranger. You resign your privacy when you become famous. I grew to hate it.

Two incidents made me realise that it was worthwhile. One

happened in the Music Hall in Aberdeen, that cold north-east city with its reputation for immovable dourness. The Aberdeen Music Hall was packed and when I was introduced by the Chairman the audience rose and cheered. That was just par for the course. It happened all the time then. But when you are on a platform looking down at a sea of faces you seldom focus on any one person. I managed to. It was on an elderly man who was waving his cap in the air and tears were running down his face.

The other incident was at the ferry at North Ballachulish. As I drove down the road towards the slip I passed three ladies who were walking up from the ferry. They had aprons on so they had probably crossed the ferry from their work at the hotel on the south shore. One of them shouted, 'That's Ian Hamilton', and turned and ran all the way back down to where I had stopped my car in the ferry queue. We gazed at one another shyly, neither of us knowing what to say. Then we shook hands in silence and she ran back to her friends. As she did so I heard her call to them, 'It was him. It was him'. If I entered into the hearts of ordinary people like that, then I had done something worth while. But I think people expected me to go on doing things almost daily, and it is not easy to keep going like that. It was a year or two before I was able to make another gesture, however small.

Keeping going is the lesson to be learned from Scottish history. If it was anything of significance, the Stone of Destiny was a set-piece battle. We Scots are not good at set piece battles. We have lost too many of them. That is why winning one now and again does so much for our morale. We always hope to win, but expect to lose. Enduring is the thing. Just going on being Scots, and damning the consequences, and damning those in every generation who sell out and go over to the other side. Without bombs, without violence without hatred, although it is difficult sometimes not to hate the Quislings, we must plod along. The Scottish race was here, under whatever name, long before the English were woad-painted savages. It reached a low ebb in the early twentieth century, but the tide has turned, and the flood now flows.

Was the Stone worth taking, now that it is back at Westminister under a secure, and perhaps impossibly strong guard? I answer that question, first of all with a story. A few years ago my wife took our son Stewart to Westminster Abbey to see the Stone of Destiny. It is behind bars. Stewart, aged ten, stretched his hand as far as his arm would reach to try to touch the talisman of his people. He could not reach it. But he got the idea, both about the Stone and about his country. So long as the Stone is behind bars in England it is a niggle to the Scottish conscience. If I were an English statesman I would worry about the Scottish conscience. You never know when it is going to take afront.

History is ideas. Events are their manifestation. We made manifest an idea. Oh yes. It was worth doing.

6 The Faculty of Advocates

AFTER THE STONE OF DESTINY affair my life could have been all plain sailing. I could have gone into one of the multi-national companies, got a company car and an expense account and become an executive. Most of my friends from the University did that. This would have cost me my freedom, and all my life that has been very precious to me. I soldiered on on my own instead. I have been in debt, in love and in trouble ever since, but I have been my own person, with whatever advantages of freedom of conscience that brings to a man or a nation.

My activities at Westminster happened in the year of the fifth centenary of Glasgow University. King George VI and Queen Elizabeth, now the Queen Mother, were due to take part in the celebrations, but they cancelled their visit, giving no reason. One can make a good guess, one can. The Stone is said to have cost the Principal of the University, Sir Hector Hetherington his peerage. It cost me my arts degree. Despite all my examination passing techniques I was so often ploughed in Honours Economics, about which I knew nothing and cared less, that I had to leave with only a law degree. I left with something more precious than an arts degree. I left with a fiancee.

Earlier I made passing mention of my mis-spent youth. Sheila Fenwick was not part of the mis-spending. She came from Sunderland and was an only child of a widow. Sheila's people make lemonade. A more douce, quiet, respectable, English family it would be impossible to imagine, and it was their misfortune that this only child fell in love with me, and I with her. She lit up a room for me every time she came into it, yet she was conventional and sought nothing more than security and a quiet life. Why nature paired us is a great mystery. Yet our three children are proof of nature's wisdom.

A Touch of Treason

Luck has followed me all the days of my life, because I have felt things deeply, and the love of a man for a woman is one of these things which has seized me beyond any hope of redemption. The world is well lost for the loves I have had. I have been deeply in love twice, and these loves have been the principal things in my life.

We did our early impressing of one another on the islands on Loch Lomond. Every February, then as now, an itch comes into my blood when the first blackbird sings and I long to get away to the lonely places. For me who had always been alone and never had a friend of my own age it was an enchantment to take her to these secret places that I knew and loved. In those days you could hitch-hike out to Balmaha, and hire a rowing boat from the MacFarlanes who among many other things ran the mails out to the islands. Inch Cailloch was our usual destination. On the far side from Balmaha there is a sandy bay, and in those days, apart from a monstrous capercailzie, the island was deserted. Together we lay at the edge of the trees and planned our lives. Our life together only lasted twelve years but every particle of them is a treasure.

Despite our many fights the glint of possession was in Sheila's eyes, and very glad I was to be possessed. Wherever my adventures may take me, home calls very strongly. Round about that time my book was accepted for publication. The newspaper story had been sold for the Covenant some time before, and the Covenant had got the money for that, but the book was my own. I lost my ex-serviceman's grant through neglecting my studies, and the royalties from the book came in just in time to save me and give me a breathing space before starting on the full time business of supporting a wife and family.

I had now all the qualifications to set myself up as a solicitor, or to get a job with an established firm. This would have been the wise thing to do. Whatever views I hold, and however extravagantly I express them, I have always treated the bench with the respect that is due to the judiciary in any society, and I have reaped what I have sown. I could have made my mark quite quickly in the Sheriff Courts as I was to do after an interval in the Court of Session. There was however the senior branch of the profession to be considered, and that seemed a long way above a tailor's son with a broad Paisley accent, which I had no intention of changing. In the 1950s membership of the Faculty of Advocates was reserved for the landed gentry, and the sons of judges. There were a few people who got in by aping such people and lying quiet until they were accepted. You had to buy your way in, like buying a commission last century in the Brigade of Guards. Putting a price on entry was designed to keep out riff-raff like myself. I got there as a pirate. It cost me £450, and if I had not taken the Stone I would never have been able to afford to become an advocate.The royalties from my book provided the entry money.

The Faculty of Advocates, as the Scottish Bar is called is a remarkable body. I joined it because I had a compulsion to be at the top, and like all shot-gun unions it led to a love-hate relationship, until quite suddenly I was able to accept enough of its terms to get by. It has accepted some of mine, although my refusal to see my life as bounded by the four walls of the Parliament House and by its conventions, as well as a certain outspokenness of tongue has led many to shun my company. My closer friends have from time to time formed a save-Ian-from-himself squad to try to promote my interests, but it is no use. Conformity out of court is beyond me.

Most advocates think that the earth revolves round them and that Parliament House is the centre of the universe. Up until 1532 the Scottish Courts were peripatetic, that is they had no fixed place of session. The law courts were part of the royal court and went wherever the king decided to reside, however temporarily. Although Edinburgh was the nominal capital, political and social factors dictated that the royal court had to go elsewhere. A show of armed force, pageantry, or the simple charm of the Stewart monarchy often made it desirable for the king to be seen in places far from Edinburgh. Above all was the compelling poverty of medieval times. When the Court stayed too long in one place it ate the surrounding countryside bare.

If the Courts of Justice were not permanently in one place the litigant would not know where to go. A litigant from Dumfries might come to Edinburgh to find that the Royal Court had crossed the water to Dunfermline, ever a popular place with the Stewart kings. On crossing the ferry, he might find that the Court had moved on. It must have been a frustrating method of seeking redress. James V changed all that. He decreed that a court should be in permanent session in Edinburgh to hear civil cases, and from its permanency of session it is to this day called the Court of Session, and only advocates can appear before it. Advocates likewise can only appear before the High Court which tries serious crime, not merely in Edinburgh, but in the nearest large town or city to where the crime has been committed. This forces advocates to leave their cosy little quarters in Parliament House. 'Going on circuit', they call it.

Parliament House lies behind St Giles Cathedral in Edinburgh. When the Scottish Parliament voted itself out of existence in 1707 it left its home empty. The Courts moved in. Court dress was laid down by James VI who stated specifically that it was to impress lay people. It still does. If we lawyers were allowed a personal preference it would be for a less fussy outfit, and for one which is more comfortable to wear, and less bulky to carry when we go on circuit. Apart from actors we are the only people who wear a wig to work. You soon get very attached to it, and it to you. It smells. It is considered unlucky to wash it, and if your wife sneaks it away and cleans it, it all bumbles up and you can do nothing with it. It is a short-sided wig with curls and two pig-tails. When an advocate scores a point off an opponent you may see him flick the pig-tail from the back of his neck. That may mean simply that it is tickling him. More often it is the court equivalent of the two-fingered gesture. A new wig costs about £400.

As well as a wig junior counsel wears a stuff gown. Senior counsel wear the same wig. Only on ceremonial occasions and in the House of Lords do they wear the full-bottomed wig, which hangs down to the shoulders, and gets in your soup like a spaniel's ears. Senior counsel wear a silk gown, hence the phrase, 'taking silk'. You get to be a silk by survival and by being a good boy and being good at your job. A silk's commission is still signed by the Queen's own hand. Since I am a silk you will observe a certain irony here. People can be generous in high places as well as in low. Contrary to popular belief we advocates don't take our court dress all that seriously. I think the public like it. From our point of view it is a useful disguise. I've stood beside many a witness in a canteen queue, after I have disrobed, and heard them discuss me. They haven't always liked me, so it is a good thing that in court I looked different. Judges wear smashing robes, and look great. They are real people underneath.

The public should take a deep breath and decide whether they want people or civil servants as their judges. Civil servants are trained mice. Judges are human. Every now and again one of them lifts a lawless leg and the newspapers go into a great paroxysm of morality. Next month some judge discloses ignorance of the name of the heroine of a soap opera, and the same newspapers say the bench is detached from life. I prefer an adulterous fornicating drunken sort of chap as a judge, who knows his job, to a dweller in a monastery, as most sinners would. I am not saying there are any like that on the Scottish Bench, but no one wants saints either. Other societies have had as their judges the utterly pure. They were called eunuchs, and castration of candidates for the bench may be the answer. But we might lose a lot of abilities along with the judicial functions. Some of them might refuse high judicial office at that price. We should, of course have women judges. Few women want to be judges. They have more sense, and more to do with their lives than to sit up there to be persuaded and flattered. The career is open to them. None has chosen it so far. Don't blame us men. I could name the first woman who is going to be appointed a judge. She is a splendid person, but so modest that she would be affronted at being named. She's fierce as well.

Judges have always been recruited from among the most senior Queen's Counsel, and the appointment limits their basic freedom. I want to be free to go to public houses, gay bars, discos, and massage parlours without let or hindrance, and to write books like this. I value the freedom of being trundled home at three o'clock in the morning in a wheel-barrow, preceded by a piper. I may not excercise all these freedoms, but I value them. I alone lay down the parameters of my social behaviour, not the Lord President of the Court of Session, not the Dean of the Faculty of Advocates, and not the editor of any journal, however popular. When I became an advocate I did not surrender my conscience to any other lawyer, and certainly not to a journalist. I would not be fit to advise my fellow citizens if I had. Since I am unwilling to answer for my social conduct at the bar of public opinion I am unfit to be a judge, nor do I want to be one. But I know the mysterious goings on before the white smoke curls from the Lord Advocate's chimney and all the advocates standing in Heriot Row stamp their feet and shout *Habemus Papa*.

From a very early age aspirants are watched. They are watched by their colleagues, and by the bench. That is all. In a small country nothing could be simpler or better. The founding fathers of the American Republic, many of whom were Scots, wrongly thought that new Scottish judges were selected by the bench of judges, and some wanted that system imported into the newly formed United States. There is a manuscript in the Library of Congress which says so. There are many Americans, watching the right wing lurch of American domestic policies who now wish that that system had been adopted. Who better is there to say who will make good judges than those men who are hearing and seeing the future candidates day and daily? As this will very shortly include solicitors, I cannot see why people gripe. Do they want priests or ex-moderators of the Free Church? For my part, the only change I would make is to bar the Lord Advocate from ever becoming a judge. Politics should play no part in the judicial selection process. The prime function of the bench is to act as moderator between the state and the individual, not to fiat the orders of Parliament. The Nuremburg trials put an end to the rule that we must always do what our rulers tell us to do. The defence of 'superior orders' is no part of the Law of Scotland, even if the superior orders come from Parliament itself.

I also think it is a mistake to open the Bench of the Supreme Courts to solicitors, but that is the view of one querulous and suspicious man. Under the present system anyone can become a judge. All they have to do is become a Queen's Counsel first. That means long years of lonely independence, some of the first ones spent in penury. It means having no one to tell you what to do, and being no one's lackey. It should also mean going into whatever places you want to and keeping whatever company you want to, and saying publish and be damned. Solicitors, on the other hand are perjink. Their clients expect it. They start off as employees, and end up employed by their partnerships, or worse still by the Secretary of State for Scotland. They have no training in independence. Would you like to sue the Government, knowing that the judge had, until his elevation, been the Secretary of State's employee? It may come to that yet.

Solicitors can appear without counsel in the Sheriff Court. This is a court which tries criminal cases and hears civil cases. There is no limit to the type of civil case it can hear and it tries all but the more serious criminal cases. It would be cheaper to abolish the supreme courts, and leave only the Sheriff Court. We may see that done yet. If so, the small man with the small cause is doomed. At present any solicitor in Scotland can take the advice of counsel, and pass it on to his client. If the supreme courts go, advocates go with them, and we will all be in firms in the cities. There will be no place for the general practitioner any more. All us consultants will be in partnerships which will be competing with the small firms, and we will compete them out of existence. We will say, 'Don't ask us for advice. If your client wants us he can come to us in the first place.' That will be a good thing for us. We will have security at last, and will be able to charge a great deal. All professions are a conspiracy against the public, and when we are in a monopoly we will be able to charge what we like. I don't like the idea, but if that is what the public want, we shall have to give it to them. At present we are not monopolists, but competitors, all practising from the Parliament House where our expertise is for sale.

Some interesting, and peculiarly Scottish results arise from the arrangement whereby all advocates practise from the Parliament House. Instead of each of us having an office of our own we work, when not in court, in the Advocates' Library. A solicitor, or his clerk, wishing to send us a brief must have somewhere to leave it. The problem is solved by each of us having a wooden box, about nine inches deep, by eighteen inches long by a foot across. These are our shop windows. A brass plate with our name on it is on the front. These boxes are kept at all times on long wooden trestles running along the walls of the principal corridors adjacent to Parliament Hall. Each box has a lid. An open lid does not necessarily denote the presence of an advocate in the Parliament House as someone may have opened it for him. But there is always something sinister about a closed lid. Despite the fact that these boxes contain all the secrets of an advocate's clients no advocate would read what is in another advocate's box. There has been no known breach of trust. That simple statement says something for the professional standard expected and delivered from a member of the Faculty of Advocates of Scotland. In these days of Watergate scandals we are not being naive. Honesty is still practised amongst us, and there are always security men to see that no outsider interferes. For all I may say about the Faculty of Advocates, I am proud to belong to it.

Since most advocates work at home as well as in the Courts some means of transporting our papers to our houses had to be found. A gentleman does not carry anything more than an umbrella and a sense of his own importance, so a bagman is employed. He transports our papers between our houses, (those who have them and I am no longer one of them) in the New Town of Edinburgh, where by tradition advocates reside. Every evening in term time the bagman goes round the boxes and puts the papers from each box into a canvas bag with the advocate's name on it and this is delivered to the advocate's house. The process is reversed in the morning.

In the 1950s the service was performed by Willie Scoon, who had succeeded his father and by the time he retired he and his father had served the Faculty for a combined total of a hundred years. When I first took the bag service Willie Scoon pushed the bags in a hand barrow and one winter's morning he collapsed in the street from some malady which fortunately did not prove fatal. He was the sort of man who would go on serving until he dropped, and when he dropped the whole administration of justice in the supreme courts of Scotland jolted to a halt. No advocate had his papers that morning. A society which can attract service like that cannot be altogether bad. He groomed a successor who drove a van and him also I know and admire. Advocates are not the only people who serve the Parliament House.

The Faculty comes in for a great deal of stick and will now

get some from me. As Norman F. Dixon points out in his work, *On the Psychology of Military Incompetence*, people of an authoritarian nature are attracted to a rigid career structure and the anonymity of a uniform. The wig and gown, and the steady upward progress towards the bench inevitably attracts some such persons to the Parliament House. They come with a simple name like William Brown and in two seconds flat have become Bill Khaki-Browne. Having thus established their superior status with a claw-hammer name, they set themselves up as the military police of the profession, and fire off complaints about their fellows. 'Dear Dean, I was appalled', their letters begin. You could paper a wall with them. A few years in the Parliament House usually cure such arrogance.

Arrogance is probably the greatest sin of the Faculty, as it is of any body of people set aside by the narrow nature of its work. The high educational qualifications make the Faculty feel that it is a sort of civilian Brigade of Guards. Yet for all its faults I find myself defending it when I had expected to be attacking it. The standard of its forensic skill is immeasurably higher than anything I have heard elsewhere or read of in quite a wide range of reading. Our oral pleading by means of stating a premise followed by deductions from that premise, is, I am told by visiting jurists, unique and much envied. The fact that Scots Law comes from a number of basic premises has lent itself to a form of pleading which is as old as Socrates. The Faculty has produced some men of world class outside the law. Walter Scott and David Hume are the best examples. David Hume was not an advocate, but he was our librarian. Our jurists are studied abroad more intimately than they are studied in our own law schools. Apart from Scots law I am trained in the English legal tradition, being also a Canadian barrister, and from my studies in English law I know that Baron Hume, on crime is a unique Scottish contribution to world criminal jurisprudence. 'It is not Holy Writ', as Lord Justice Clerk Wheatley once observed to me in the Appeal Court, 'but we will take a lot of persuading to go against it.'

The Faculty, so often accused of grasping meanness is capable of wild acts of generosity. Until the introduction of criminal legal aid in 1964 it provided totally free legal representation in all criminal cases in the High Court. In the most serious cases a busy silk would send back his lucrative civil work without hesitation and without any reward, except the satisfaction of helping a fellow citizen in trouble. Prior to the introduction of legal aid for civil cases in 1948 it provided free legal assistance for poor litigants in certain classes of cases, including divorce. In 1922 when the immensely valuable library became too large for the Faculty properly to handle, it handed it over to the nation to found the National Library of Scotland. Predictably the nation, represented by Westmister, refused it, but a public subscription was raised and made it available to the public. Even today our great library of law books may be consulted free through the National Library of Scotland to anyone who is conducting his own litigation, or who merely wants to inform himself in some bye-way of legal studies. The Faculty, for all its age does not own any silver, not even a teaspoon. It is a glory for a small nation to have provided humanity with one of the greatest libraries in the world, and at the same time to have disdained the collection of knick-knacks.

7 Elizabeth I versus Elizabeth II

ADVOCATES FILLED the social void left by the Members of Parliament when they went south in 1707. In the 1950s quite a few advocates were there only for social reasons. They were never let loose on a case. Nowadays most practising advocates come from very much the same background as I do, but that was not so then. Even the ones whose background was solid but humble were keen to conceal it. All aped the English public school tradition, particularly the egregious one of addressing each other by the surname, without any honorific, a practice which every Scot finds offensive. Dollies many of them were, but not without their amusing attributes.

There were some real oddities. Gordon Brown, the head Faculty Servitor was not one of them. Note well the word Servitor. It is not a fancy name for a janitor. The head Servitor looks after all the day-to-day running of the Faculty staff who keep the place clean, and do everything from marshalling a procession, to sewing on a fly button which has come off just before an important appearance in the Appeal Court. Gordon Brown and his father, like Willie Scoon and his, had given a combined service of a hundred years to the Faculty so he knew everything about the Parliament House. Mr Brown's service had been broken by a greater service with the Royal Air Force in wartime. He had been a senior NCO in charge of aircraft maintenance. Our common interest in aircraft brought us to a greater intimacy than was usual between advocate and Servitor, and from time to time I heard comments on my brother advocates to which, strictly speaking, I should not have listened.

At that time we had not yet taken any hasty or untoward steps into the twentieth century which was only a little over fifty years old. Thus among us the electric telephone was not greatly in use. Indeed there were only three of them in the whole building, and each of them was a pre-payment coin box. There were then only four advocates clerks and they shared one such telephone. Each so mistrusted the others that he kept his own little pile of pennies in a drawer in his desk. At that time you put two pennies in the slot, dialled the number and when it answered pressed button A. If it did not answer you pressed button B and got your money back. This was as simple an example of the law of contract as anyone could devise. It was too much for one Queen's Counsel. He could not differentiate button A from button B. On connection with his number he would press button B, be cut off, and get his money back. Worse. When his number had rung out so that there was no reply he would press button A and lose his tuppence. This he regarded as a typical exactment of a malign socialist influence which he believed darkly was everywhere at work.

The two telephone boxes for use of Members of Faculty were situated next to Mr Brown's glass cubicle just off Parliament Hall. Mr Brown, as ever helpful, used to make this gentleman's connection for him, even to the extent of exercising the not too difficult choice between button A and button B.

'You know, Brown,' said the Queen's Counsel after one such occasion. 'It is strange how an educated person such as I am can never get that thing to work, while an unlettered fellow like yourself has no trouble with it.'

Mr Brown accepted the remark with humorous resignation. When Mr Brown retired in 1982 and was succeeded by Mr Manson, a former Naval Chief Petty Officer, there was a faction in the Faculty who wanted him to change his name to Brown, in order either to preserve historical continuity or to save the mental exercise of memorising a new name. Other counsels prevailed over this delightful piece of madness. Mr Manson has settled entirely into the role and is the perfect Servitor. I suppose that his naval career has helped to prepare him for the service of madmen, yet whiles I see a certain glint in his eye and when I do I would give much to know what he is thinking.

Advocates, like jockeys have difficulty in looking after themselves. Like jockeys we have valets, whom we call robers to assist us into our court gear. I once counted that it takes thirty-seven separate items of clothing to get a Queen's Counsel into court, not counting the watch and chain which I don't wear. In a busy morning in the robing room, with upwards of fifty counsel changing into wig and gown, and all doing it at the last minute before court, it is a hectic scene. There is very little turn-over among the robers who seem to go on for ever. They must like the job and certainly many is the time I would go into court unwigged, or with my flies open if they were not there to see me properly dressed. However nonchalant we appear in court there is a ferment underneath. I have never risen to cross-examine an important witness or to address a jury without my heart pounding and a sweat breaking out over me, and this causes a certain detachment and lack of concentration on such matters as robing for court. Robers are among the great unseen assistants to any forensic fight.

No account of the Faculty of the 1950s should fail to mention the first two lady members of Faculty. You will note the description. 'Lady'; no woman has yet become an advocate. Miss Kidd, the first lady advocate and later Dame Margaret Kidd, was a delightful gentle creature and the mere insistence on her right to enter a male preserve showed singleness of purpose and sheer courage. It is difficult to imagine today just how necessary these qualities then were. Women were not expected to plead, and if they did then they were expected to do so in a lady-like manner, different, and therefore inferior to the way a man would do it. This was the attitude from great oafs who could not use a telephone and needed a chauffeur to drive a car. Yes. Several advocates arrived every morning in great chauffeur-driven cars, so long that they needed an intercom between the back seat and the driver. I never saw one of these russet-faced gentry in court but they appeared in the advocates' luncheon room, holding forth about their unreported cases, and hoisting in great forkfuls of food, each bite chewed forty times as though being considered for judgment.

Miss Kidd contented herself with being admitted to the Faculty. She never fought the ranks of privilege the way the next lady member fought and won. Isobel Sinclair had been a journalist and she was as determined to earn a living at pleading as she had done with her pen. She was also determined to assert her rights to all the social aspects of the Parliament House. She turned over new ground like a plough and like a plough she turned up many worms. Isobel Sinclair was a vital young woman and in that den of elderly men of all ages she was regarded with consternation. Of course there was no question of her sharing a robing room with gentlemen members of Faculty. I don't know what they thought would happen to them or her if she did. In Edinburgh our ladies are still segregated from us in some far distant room, regardless of the fact that on circuit we all get along happily in one room without anything untoward happening. Edinburgh is like that. A rearguard action was fought over Isobel's insistence that she was going to use the lunch room. This right was denied to her on what grounds I know not. With great bravery, on the first day of her calling to the Bar she marched in and sat down. She won, and after that had only one further battle to fight.

Trifling as the matter was, it was a famous victory for women's rights. One day she made her first appearance in the Appeal Court. She was wearing red nail varnish. Lord President Cooper was a great gentlemen, and either out of tact or from the discretion which salts all elderly bachelors when dealing with young women he said nothing, but called in the Dean of Faculty and put upon him the task of telling Isobel that red nail varnish was not consonant with the dignity of an advocate appearing at the bar of the Appeal Court. The Dean was Sir John Cameron, universally known as Jock. Awful, solemn, unpompous, terrible, and loved, he became the most distinguished of judges.

Jock took thought and on a suitable morning invited Isobel to pace the hall with him. Advocates are wont to pace up and down in the Parliament Hall when they are waiting for their cases to be called, and it is a great honour for a young advocate to be seen walking the Hall with the Dean of Faculty. Up and down they went. The great advocate, and the newly called little lady. At last Jock worked the conversation round to the offending subject and suggested that it might, just might, be a good idea if Isobel cleared that stuff off her nails. So outraged was Isobel that she forgot the greatness of the occasion and turned on Jock with the fury of a young woman insulted. 'I will take off my nail varnish, if you will take off these silly side-whiskers you've recently started growing,' she said, and walked away in horror at her temerity. Jock did. Isobel didn't.

That was the last battle and ladies now come and go in the Parliament House without let or hindrance. I have often wondered how Jock reported back to Lord Cooper, but they were both great human beings, and I expect that they had a quiet laugh at themselves and respected Isobel all the more for her stance. I hope Jock and she do not mind my telling this story. I had it from Isobel many years ago, and the present generation of lady members should know about it and give Isobel a dinner. She won their freedom for them.

I have mentioned my Paisley accent, and accents are only interesting by comparison. Parliament House has its own, and no one hearing it is ever likely to forget it. A small community, repressed, anglicised, professional, its members earning their livelihood by the spoken word, is likely to develop certain mannerisms and modes of speech. When the society socialises very much within itself its accent becomes associated with an almost tribal sense of propriety which would have delighted

Malinowski. It is impossible in the written word to convey any true sense of the Parliament House accent but the only other body who would take to it naturally are the civil servants at the Ministry of Funny Walks. It is the verbal equivalent.

Not so long ago I was appearing before a judge who is the greatest exponent of Parliament House-speak. The case concerned a young woman with whom my client had had brief sexual congress, so brief that it was suggested that the young lady had not entirely been a consenting party. In an adjacent room to this event was a man called Willie, his wife and a baby. The wife was a star witness for the defence.

'Naw. Naw,' she said. 'Yon wusny rape. Fyon adav bin rape shwudav woke oor Wullie an the wean, so shwudav an shdidny.'

His Lordship attempted to put this into what he assumed was basic English for the benefit of the jury, but Parliament House-speak failed lamentably to convey the indignation of the witness, and his attempt was misconstrued. As the jury went out I heard one juror say to her neighbour, 'Ahm no fur dain whit yon poncy-voiced auld bastard up ther wants us tae dae. Ahm fur letting him aff,' and this the jury duly did. Glasgow and Parliament House belong to different civilisations.

It was into this rarified community of the Parliament House that I projected myself in the spring of 1953 to commence my devilling. Yet before I was called to the Bar factors were to arise which nearly stopped me from becoming an advocate, and which certainly made my start in practice much more difficult. These factors were precipitated by the death of King George VI on 6 February 1952. On his death his daughter Elizabeth was proclaimed Queen under the title of Elizabeth II, a numeral which caused great offence in Scotland. There never has been a prior Elizabeth of Scotland and 'the numeral' as it came to be called suggested that Scotland had been absorbed by England. It is natural and understandable that England

83

would want to be reminded of its great Elizabethan age, when piracy was elevated to a national pastime. A degree of piracy in my own nature has made me delight in Elizabethan England. What surprised me was the degree of feeling among the people of Scotland, who have never been remarkable in showing any deep feeling for their country's past. They did now. Scotland was affronted.

When the new title was announced objections were voiced all over Scotland. When the proclamation of the accession was made at the Mercat Cross outside St Giles there were cries of protest from the crowd. The matter did not end there. When shops and stores were decked out in preparation for the coronation anything having the numeral was torn down. It went so far that human ladders were formed, umbrellas passed up to the person at the top, and the offending decoration hooked down. Government can only be conducted with the consent of the governed, but it takes a long time to get even an elementary idea into the brain of the English, and since English nationalism was involved, the numeral was foisted on an unwilling Scotland. The lame, the weak, the halt would not bend, but the Scottish MPs bowed deeply. They all swore allegiance to Elizabeth 'the Second'.

The first public manifestation of the Goverment's intransigence was a new pillar box. It bore the hated numeral 'E II R'. It was erected in the Inch housing scheme in Edinburgh and was repeatedly defaced, replaced, defaced and replaced until finally it was blown up. This is the first time that explosives have effectively been used to further a Scottish cause since the 1745 rebellion. I didn't do it. In these matters I am led by Mahatma Gandhi who freed a sub-continent with a poke of salt. My way is more effective, and lasting. Having spurned all lawful protest the Government weakly gave in to this one, and no further boxes were erected with the numeral, although until recently post office vans still carried them. There is something personal about a van. It has a driver in it.

They went unscathed. To this day two types of pillar boxes are made, and only the English ones have the numeral.

In these far off days, at the start of the reign of Elizabeth, the monarchy was treated with a mystical reverence as though they were not the Royal Family, but the Holy Family. Her Majesty's reference in one of her early speeches to, 'my illustrious ancestress Queen Elizabeth,' did much to encourage this view. Descent from a virgin queen, forsooth. There's only been one other descent like it in history. The Scottish tradition, when we had sovereigns of our own, was to treat them very much as ordinary people, which is what they are. Their title was much more humble, as befitted a sovereign who was first among equals, not a conqueror. Your Grace. Never the flattering, Your Majesty. And our sovereigns were Kings of Scots, Kings of the people, not the territory. The English tradition, stemming from the Norman conquest, is to treat them with an adulation not found outside Hymns Ancient and Modern and Songs of Praise.

As a result John MacCormick and I had to go warily on the Queen's title issue. We could not have written the paragraph I have written above. We would have been lynched. Besides, John tried to court public opinion, and I don't give a damn for it. Nowadays businessmen would have supplied the popular demand for royal trivia by bringing out a series of coronation souveniers, bearing the title Elizabeth the First, Second to None, but in these days it was too hot to handle. John MacCormick and I had to do it ourselves. Until it was seen that we would not be struck down by fire from heaven for our impiety, we had difficulty in finding manufacturers to take our orders. Although they reported our actions in their news columns the national press refused to take our advertisements. I would like to report that we became rich. We didn't. Despite the demand, none of the ordinary retail outlets would stock our goods and we had to sell them through the branches of the Covenant Association, and the Association took all the profits.

I expect that somewhere some of these souveniers still lurk in some bottom drawer, but I am a disperser rather than a collector and mine have long since gone. A more serious matter than mere souveniers also took up our attention.

One fine pring day in 1953, John MacCormick and I went out to Loch Lomondside and took my copy of the standard work on the British constitution with us. One of the subjects which we had constantly raised in our many discussions was the status of the Treaty of Union between Scotland and England. The English view is that their Government can do anything, the typical view of a conquered people. In the Forces my fellows used to say, 'They can even make you have a baby. The only thing they can't do is make you love the bastard.' We did not think this was the law. We set out to show that the powers of Parliament were limited. It must at least be bound by the limits of the Treaty of Union between the two countries, we argued. In the royal title we had a vehicle to challenge the power of Parliament in the courts. We did not think that we would win on the issue itself, and indeed we did not care. What we wanted to do was to challenge the arrogant assumption, that notwithstanding the solemn treaty entered into between Scotland and England in 1707, that Treaty could be ignored. It was a brave challenge from two men, one a practising solicitor, and the other a law student, determined to attack a political theory which went to the very root of English constitutional government. I am proud to have played my part.

MacCormick and another against the Lord Advocate is the leading case on Scottish Constitutional Law yet we had great difficulty in getting it into court. In order to present a case in the Court of Session it is necessary to have the services of an Edinburgh solicitor. None of the established firms would touch our case. Finally we hit on Donald MacNeil MacWilliam, a Mulloch who had recently set up on his own and who needed the money badly enough to brave the unknown terrors that all others shied from. John MacCormick pled his own case in court, and my devil-master John Bayne argued my case for me. We got short shrift before Lord Guthrie in the Outer House, and however much we had accepted that this was bound to happen it was a bitter lonely time. We expected the Appeal Court to hit us for six.

The Appeal was held before three judges with the late Lord President Cooper in the Chair. Lord Cooper was a Scottish historian, and it is said of him that during the course of his whole adult life he never read a book that was not either a history book or a law book. Scotland being Scotland a sardonic remark had to be coined about him. This was that the historians said that he was a fine lawyer, and that the lawyers said that he was a fine historian. In fact he was both. His translation of the Declaration of Arbroath is the standard against which all others are measured.

On the day of the Appeal we knew that we would get a fair hearing, but we also knew that we were challenging long established principles and that we might have to leave court with our heads high and our hearts lower than they had ever been. There were so few of us in those days. John opened our Appeal and was heard in polite silence. It is one of the most disconcerting things when a pleader receives no comment from the bench. He has no idea how his argument is being received or what the judges are thinking and there comes a time when any interruption is welcome. It seemed to me that John was merely being accorded the silence that is always given to someone presenting his own case, however hopeless. When John Bayne got up to act as sweeper and to present my case, which was of course identical to John's, a few questions were put to him, but on the whole we seemed to be getting no more than a polite and hostile reception.

Our spirits rose however when the Lord Advocate rose to reply. The Lord Advocate then was James Letham Clyde a man who was never popular among his peers. He later became

Lord President and contributed a lot to Scots law but his somewhat sneering attitude to those about him, which probably only concealed diffidence and shyness, made him seem hostile to his fellows. His opening words brought a stinging rebuke from Lord Cooper.

'I am not here,' said the Lord Advocate, 'to make a political speech and to turn this court into the hustings.'

'Even if you were to try, Lord Advocate,' observed the Lord President,'we would not permit you.'

From then on the three judges put each point raised by John MacCormick to the Lord Advocate, forcing concessions here, and making observations there, until it was clear that they had noted our case, and were giving keen attention to it all.

John was called on to reply. I well remember his closing words which I knew to be directed at the jammed audience in the public benches, rather than to the court itself.

'It is asserted that this old country of Scotland has ceased to exist,' he said, 'and that may be the legal position. Nevertheless it has not been absorbed into England, and we bring this action on behalf of our country before its highest tribunal to vindicate its rights.'

We lost the action but won from the Court an important Opinion on the constitutional position of Scotland. It was the position we had reached in our long discussions and which at our meeting on Loch Lomondside we had agreed jointly to advance. I quote the following few sentences from the judgment of Lord Cooper.

'The principle of the unlimited Sovereignty of Parliament is a distinctively English principle which has no counterpart in Scottish Constitutional law. . . Considering that the Union legislation extinguished the Parliaments of Scotland and England, and replaced them by a new Parliament, I have difficulty in seeing why it should have been supposed that the new Parliament of Great Britain must inherit all the peculiar characteristics of the English Parliament but none of the

Scottish Parliament, as if all that had happened in 1707 was that the Scottish representatives were admitted to the Parliament of England. That is not what was done.'

There was a sequel to this Opinion. The judgment of the court was delivered at a later date and the question of expenses had to be considered. In the usual way the losing side pays the expenses of the other side. The Lord Advocate sent his Home Advocate Depute, Gordon Thomson, later Lord Migdale into court to move for expenses against John and me.

'I am instructed to move for expenses against the appellants,' he said.

Lord Cooper observed, 'When an advocate says that he is instructed to do something, my experience is that he does not agree with his instructions.'

To which Gordon Thomson replied, 'I am instructed to move for expenses against the appellants.'

Lord Cooper made the order of the Court. 'In respect that this action was brought in the public interest by two gentlemen of Scotland we shall make no order of expenses against the appellants.'

I wonder if he knew just how much these words meant to a young lawyer about to set out on his career.

I would like to write that that was the end of the matter, and from then on I was a tee-ed ball, ready to soar down the fairway of my career. Things have never happened like that to me. The decision of the Court of Appeal was given on 30 July 1953. By the following summer I had passed all my examinations, concluded my devilling and was ready to be called to the Bar. There was however one further hurdle. Since 1745 all advocates have been required on being called to the Bar to take an oath of loyalty to the Crown, and this oath now included the numeral. Having been one of the litigants in the Queen's title action I was expected to refuse to take the oath to Elizabeth II and to make a scene in open court when I was called forward to the Bar to be sworn in.

I had other views. It seemed to me that I had done enough in this matter. I had worked hard. I was due to be married, and I wanted nothing more than to to be allowed to settle down and to get on with my private life. It was not as simple as that. Somewhere in a Sean O'Casey play a character protests, 'Surely I've done enough for Ireland,' to which he gets the uncompromising reply, 'No man can do enough for Ireland.' I found myself in the same position. A principle is a principle. They stick like burrs. Mine stuck and I indicated that I would refuse to take the oath in its then form. This decision was immediately conveyed by my devil master to the Dean of Faculty.

The Dean is the head of the Faculty of Advocates, and its ruling figure. He is elected by the Members of Faculty who thereafter support him solidly. His authority is ancient and unchallenged. His office dates from medieval times, and even the baton he carries on cerimonial occasions was made in the year of the Massacre of Glencoe. The Dean of Faculty when i was called to the bar was Sir John Cameron, loved, respected, and feared. If he had spoken from a burning bush it would not have terrified me more. He sent a message through my devil master that, 'If Hamilton won't take the oath of allegience in proper form he cannot become an advocate.'

There is no one to turn to on such occasions. Some people will goad you on. These are the people who would gape at a suicide. Others tell you not to be a fool. You have a responsibility to the girl you are about to marry, and you have done enough damage to your career.These are the friends truly trying to help you. No one can. There are times when it is each man for himself.

I sent the message back up the line through my devil master to the Dean that I was unmoved on the matter. From there it went to the Lord President of the Court of Session. I do not know if it went any further than that. There is not much further it can go.

On 16 July 1954 I processed behind the Dean into the court whose proceedings were summarily interrupted to take my oath. It was administered without the offensive and offending numeral. It was in the following form:

'I, Ian Robertson Hamilton swear by Almighty God that I will bear a true allegiance to Her Majesty Queen Elizabeth, Her heirs and successors according to law.'

Without the numeral it was an oath of allegiance to the people of Scotland. I took it proudly and I have kept it loyally, yet it allows me to keep a touch of treason in my heart to Her Majesty's Government at Westminster. It was more even than that. For the first time since 1707 it was an acknowledgment in constitutional law that the monarchy is not a single monarchy, but a dual monarchy. Elizabeth II, Queen of England. Elizabeth, Queen of Scots. That day Scotland recovered its separate sovereign. Tomorrow its separate sovereignty. Symbols count.

There is a parchment for every royal reign which each advocate signs immediately after he has taken the verbal oath. It contains the words of the oath, written out in a flourish of calligraphy. There are two parchments for the reign of Queen Elizabeth. The first has the numeral; the second has not. The second parchment has been signed by all advocates admitted to the Scottish Bar since 16 July 1954. My name heads the second parchment.

Many years later when the Lord Justice Clerk, Lord Wheatley, retired I wrote a farewell letter to him. In reply he was kind enough to recall that it was in his court that I had taken the oath.

'The case I was hearing,' he wrote, ' was one of public interest and the public benches were full. When, on the instructions of the Lord President, I administered the oath to you without the numeral the public broke into spontaneous applause.'

I don't remember that. I must have been too nervous to notice.

8 On Criminal Circuit

IT IS ONE of the traditions of the Bar to greet each new member with a handshake and to wish him well. I gave up the tradition last year when the new advocate turned on me with understandable asperity and said, 'Ian, that's the third time you've congratulated me and I've been at the Bar eleven years.' I am so much on circuit and there are now so many of us that is difficult to keep in touch.

In 1954 there were only seventy of us in practice and it was a neat little closed shop. I entered it with the feeling that I had arrived at last. I hadn't. It takes years to make an advocate. Furthermore law is a careful profession. To start by breaking into an Abbey, and to follow that up by suing the Lord Advocate and refusing to take the oath in proper form was inauspicious. People who want to get on should be more careful. I walked the floor of the Parliament House, up and down the long hall, gown swinging as I turned at the end, sometimes on my own, sometimes with Alastair MacDonald, now Sheriff of Shetland and one of the most mordant wits ever to don a wig and gown. Every half hour I sidled past my box to see if there was a brief in it. There wasn't. Civil work was for the established, and in the 1950s there was only the very occasional criminal case.

Since they were unpaid there was no great competition for criminal cases. One came my way two months after I was called. It was almost the only thing I did in my first year at the Bar. It was my first appearance in any court of any kind, and it was to defend a man on a charge of assault to severe injury, which in those days attracted a sentence of seven years in prison. The trial was held in the North Court in the old High Court building in the Salt Market in Glasgow. It is still my favourite forum.

With no money to pay anyone the quality of preparation of

a criminal brief was minimal. When we got to the circuit court we asked the Clerk of Court for a copy of the Indictment, as the charge sheet is called, met the client, found out what defence he had if any, and went in at the deep end. Murder was different. A Queen's Counsel, assisted by junior counsel was then instructed, and some preparation was done. The client hanged if his defence went wrong. The system is indefensible but the Crown presented their case with more gentleness than now, and while judges expected a high standard of pleading they knew the difficulties we worked under. Only the Oscar Slater case has left a stain on the memory of the days of Counsel for the Poor. Such earlier prosecutions as that of James Stewart of the Glens in 1752 and those of the two Lanarkshire weavers in 1822 were not trials at all. They were excercises in political murder.

Crown cases are prosecuted in Scotland by the Lord Advocate acting usually through his advocates depute. The advocate depute in my first trial was Gordon Gillies who later prosecuted the mass-murderer Peter Manuel. I shall not name his junior. He was about a year senior to me, and the fact that he was acting for the Crown had so gone to his head that he thought he was the Queen. I approached him that morning, to find the strength of the Crown case, something we still do even today when cases are well prepared and he said, 'You know, Hamilton, there is far too much of this sort of thing going on. People coming into court ill-prepared.' I should have kicked him in the teeth, but I didn't. The jury must have taken pity on my white wig and obvious inexperience, because they returned a verdict of not proven. Big Danny, who had had his face opened with wee Tommy's razor probably deserved all he got, and no great injustice was done.

Shortly after that, I perpetrated a grave injustice on Lord Wheatley, then one of the junior judges, later to become an awful and terrifying Lord Justice Clerk. I nearly got him arrested. It was my second and only other case in my first year and was, of course unpaid. It was in Inverness.

In those days we went on circuit by train. Regardless of expense a taxi took me to the station, where a porter trundled my bags up the platform. The train was separated into compartments, along the side of which ran a corridor. The judge travelled in lonely splendour in a compartment reserved for him. The window of the compartment bore a label saying RESERVED FOR............. and the name of the VIP. The macer took the judge's luggage separately, it being derogatory to the dignity of a judge to be seen with his baggage, and probably even with his macer. We had to change into the Glasgow-Inverness train at Perth, and I saw Lord Wheatley ahead of me looking for his reserved compartment.

'Just put my baggage in here,' I said to the porter. 'I want to avoid yon guy up ahead.'

'Is he a heid banger?' asked the porter.

I should have bitten my tongue, but words are sweeter.

'Naw,' I said. 'He's just a drunken old toff. Everytime he gets a drink in him, he kids on he's a lord.'

I settled into my compartment, well pleased with myself, and noticed with satisfaction the porter sprinting up the train to guard Lord Wheatley's compartment, against Lord Wheatley. It never occurred to me that it would cause more than a minor embarrassment, and I was filled with joy at the idea of his lordship being mistaken for a drunk. Lord Wheatley was one of the few Roman Catholics on the bench, and the first socialist. He was also a rabid Tee-totaller. No one would trace it back to me. Lord Wheatley had not, I was sure, seen me.

I was soon disabused. The train had no sooner started than the guard's voice was heard coming along the corridor.

'Mr Haaaaamilton.   Mr Haaaaamilton.' The guard gave tongue as though announcing me as the next station.

I put my face in my book but it was not a bomb-proof shelter. On his way back up the train the guard opened the door of my compartment.

'Mr Hamilton?'

I could not deny it.

'Lord Wheatley's compliments, and you're to join him in his compartment.'

The guard led me along the swaying corridor. The train was travelling fast. Would I be killed if I opened a door and hurled myself down the embankment? Would it not be better to be killed?

Off the bench Lord Wheatley was one of the pleasantest of men. He looked at me, and said almost thoughtfully, 'You know Ian it took me nearly five minutes to get that trouble sorted out on Perth Station. What did you tell them?'

I gave a much edited version, profuse with appologies.

'You nearly had me arrested.' He paused, and added. 'I suspect I'm the first of Her Majesty's judges who's had his breath sniffed for alcohol by a railway porter.' Then he chuckled, and added. 'You have well earned the lunch I propose to buy you. But don't ever do anything like that again.'

I took his advice, and never did. We had lunch together somewhere between Killiecrankie and the Slocht, but before we came to Killiecrankie the train stopped at Ballinluig Junction, where the rear two carriages were shunted off to go up the spur line to Aberfeldy. My parents lived near Ballinluig Junction, and my father had come to the platform to spend ten minutes with me, while the train waited, as Highland trains often do. We were joined by Lord Wheatley. In no time at all the old pape and the old proddy were each eating out of the other's hand, two elderly Scottish radicals deep in discussion of one of the most profound issues ever to excite the mind of mankind, well, of Scotsmankind. Was Alan Morton of Rangers, or Jimmy Delaney of Celtic the greatest man ever to kick a ball?

Even when he became a rude, and almost impossible Lord Justice Clerk, making the Appeal Court so rough to appear in that we wore jock-straps and gum shields, I always had a soft spot for Lord Wheatley. It seemed to me that I got an easier passage than most, so maybe he had a soft spot for me also.

These two cases were my first taste of the criminal law, and although I knew I had bitten off more than I could chew, the taste was sweet. It always is. Gulps are better than sips. Some criminals are evil, but some are ordinary people who have fallen into ill luck. The public think that criminal lawyers are script writers for their clients. We are no such thing. To do so is the crime of attempting to pervert the course of justice, and none of us commits it. Our job is to advance our client's side of affairs and let the jury judge. Sometimes the defence we have to put forward is ludicrous. So be it. We are not there to judge our clients, merely to defend them. And truth being much stranger than fiction, the seemingly laughable defence often stands up in court with a great deal of credibility. How do we defend someone whom we know to be guilty? We don't. Everyone is presumed to be innocent, and it is for the jury to decide the guilt, not the lawyer. My first case was a simple one, and it was to be many years before I was to lead for the defence in a murder trial.

There are few more important jobs in society than defending a fellow citizen on a charge of murder. Sitting on a jury is one of them, and I do not envy jurors their job. Most people think of a murder trial as a who dunnit, and sometimes indeed that is the case. More commonly a murder trial arises out of a fracas, and it is for the jury to decide the quality of the act. Their decision is reflected in their verdict, which can be guilty of murder, guilty of the lesser crime of culpable homicide, or an acquittal. All murder cases re-enact tragedies. There are no winners. The whole of society is the loser. I have defended many hundred over the years. One in particular still haunts me. The circumstances of it reeked of tragedy.

A young man had fallen in love with a young woman. Even in repose on the mortuary slab, she was beautiful. At a time when illegitimacy bore a stigma she had had an illegitimate child. The young man married her, and took both her and her child to his heart. He regarded the child as his own, although he knew that in blood it was not. Man and boy became bonded to one another, and both were bonded to the young woman. We debase the word love by over use, but these three were a loving trinity. They set up house. Both husband and wife worked hard, and they had a happy and secure home. Then one day things went wrong. There was a man in a high position at the woman's work, with whom she came into close contact. Perhaps from the glitter of his position, perhaps from some deeper and more creditable feeling, she fell in love with him. She decided to leave her husband and go off with this other man.

This news had to be broken to her husband, and she chose a Saturday afternoon while the boy was at play outside. Nervously she twisted and knotted a silk scarf in her hands as she broke him the news, which fell on him with shattering incredulity. He remonstrated with her, not believing this monstrous turn of fortune, and put his hands out to her. He left no mark of violence on her, but by a terrible mischance his hands had touched and compressed the cricoid cartilage in her neck. Without another word she fell dead at his feet. He tried to revive her but found her beyond revival. Then the ice-cream van sounded its horn in the street outside, and he remembered his son. He took the boy to his parents in a town some distance away, and gave himself up to the police. The scarf which his wife had been nervously knotting in her hands lay like a garrotte beside her dead body. That was the Crown's case.

It is said that much exposure to tragedy hardens a person, and this may be true. A good lawyer stands aside from his client, just as a good surgeon does. A surgeon will give the same attention to a child rapist as to a saint, and so does a lawyer. When I defend a child murderer I feel that even God has deserted him, so by God, his counsel won't. Perhaps that means that God hasn't deserted him after all. For that little man with the dead wife, I felt a terrible sympathy. It was unprofessional, but there it was.

I was instructed for the defence by Beltrami and Company, the case being prepared by James Penman, then an assistant with Beltrami, now in practice on his own. I forget at this distance of time who was my junior. When we went to see our client in Barlinnie prison we found a broken man. He had killed the woman he loved, and he was scarcely able to give coherent instructions for his defence. He had been psychiatrically examined and was certified sane and fit to plead. Bit by bit we coaxed the story from him which is narrated above.

The case for the Crown was presented by Jim Milligan QC now Lord Milligan. He presented it with great moderation, and I am glad to say that both of us concealed the name of the third member of the triangle who had precipitated the tragedy. Things went very much in favour of the defence right from the start, and from the Crown witnesses there emerged a picture of a devoted husband and father. Nevertheless, when you are fighting a murder charge there is one piece of evidence which goes very much against you. That is the colour photographs of the victim, which are the first things to go before the jury, and copies of which are retained by them throughout the trial. Pictures of a woman lying dead in her home, and then on a mortuary draining table are harrowing, and predispose a jury to convict.

The Crown case turned very much on the cause of death. The woman's knotted scarf was a damning piece of evidence. There was evidence that it could have been used to cause just the sort of injury which had proved fatal. As the picture emerged under cross-examination of the pathologists however, it became apparent that skill and knowledge would have been necessary on the part of the assailant before he could have killed with certainty in that fashion. There was no evidence to show that my client had ever had such skills, even if he had suddenly been possessed with a murderous intent. The pathologists readily conceded that such skills were of an esoteric nature, and that an unskilled killer would have left marks of violence on the body, of which there were none. The defence of accident was standing up well. It needed only my client to go into the witness-box to give his account of the affair for that defence to be made out. At this point Jim Milligan passed me a note saying that if my client was willing to plead guilty to culpable homicide, he was willing to accept that plea. I scribbled on the note that I was taking the case to the jury, and that I was going to get a full acquital. I wanted to see my client walk out of court a free man, and be reunited with his boy.

As was my duty I put the Crown's position to my client at the next adjournment, and he instructed me to plead guilty to culpable homicide. The charge still stood at murder, wrongly in my view. If the depute is willing to take a plea of guilty to culpable homicide he should not press for a conviction for murder, but that is the practice and my learned brother was doing nothing improper. I explained to my client that no reasonable jury would convict him of murder, and that the real issue was whether there had been any assault on his wife. If there had not been, and her death had been an accident, as he had told me, then he must not plead guilty. A plea of guilty meant that he had assaulted his wife and killed her. He was beyond caring what happened to him, and on his instructions I had no alternative but to return to court, sorrowfully and against my will to plead guilty to culpable homicide.

The plea was recorded, read back to the jury, and the Crown moved for sentence. It is then defence counsel's duty to plead in mitigation of the sentence about to be passed. It has been said that this bores the judge, who has already made up his mind what he is going to do anyway. This could not be further from the truth. The Judge was Lord Cameron, who as Sir John Cameron had been the Dean of Faculty of whom much has already been written. In the far off days of which I write a murder trial was still something of a rarity, and as I rose to address the court I was conscious of a great and anticipatory silence. Relatives of both the deceased and of my client were in court and for the first time they were going to hear what had happened. Two vital young people had gone into that room and only one had come out alive.

A court of law is no place for histrionics, and certainly not Lord Cameron's court. Everything has to be low key. With much practice you get to run on in advance of yourself, and to see what is going to come out long before you say it. It is as if someone else is speaking. I heard my voice narrate the facts, and as I did so I thought of the ice-cream van sounding its horn in the summer street, and it seemed to me that the whole pathos of these terrible events was illustrated by that mundane circumstance. Try as I did to avoid it I remembered the death of Mr Valiant for Truth in The Pilgrim's Progress, and how when he died all the trumpets sounded for him on the other side. When it came to describing how this young man found his wife dead at his feet, and then heard the ice-cream van I unconsciously lapsed into the first person and heard myself say, 'and then I heard the trumpet sounding in the street outside and suddenly I remembered my son.'

I corrected myself but I was much moved, and I could see that Lord Cameron was also much moved, and that he had got the allusion. With an effort we both managed to preserve our professional detachment. When I concluded my address he sentenced my client to six months in prison, back-dated to the date of his arrest. This meant that he would be released in a month's time.

That case illustrates the danger of an advocate getting too close to his client. My training carried me through, but it was a close run thing. It also illustrates the Lord Cameron I know and love. He could have had me into his side room and rebuked me for appealing to his emotions in a shameless fashion, but my action was not deliberate, as he well understood. Instead I got a little note from him, one of the many counsel have received over the years, thanking them for their pleading in a difficult case.

As for the sentence, I have often pondered on it. No advocate should ever judge his client, but I doubt if that man ever had any evil intent towards the woman he killed, and recklessness or evil intent is central to this type of crime. Yet he had pled guilty to taking her life and the law said he had to be punished. More humanely he needed time to sort himself out, and to come to the realisation that life goes on. He needed time, and in his great humanity Lord Cameron gave him just that.

An advocate's duty to his client ends when sentence is passed, but I made it my business to find out the end of the story. When the young man came out of prison he regained custody of his son.

Such meaty briefs did not come the way of junior counsel, whose row is hoed with tears and, at the beginning, with little sweat. In my first year at the Bar I earned ninety pounds. In my second eighty. Such idleness nearly drove me to distraction, but I hung on, and be damned to them. Month after month with no work was a grim experience. I know now that solicitors have the good of their clients to consider, and that nothing I had done so far could give them any confidence that I would plead ably and solidly in the courts. Then early in my third year at the Bar I looked in my box for the trillionth time and there to my astonishment was a fat brief. I took it up and shook it and read the name on it a dozen times to see that it wasn't for someone else, unable to believe it was really for me.

It was an Appeal to the Division, as we call the Appeal Court, in a case that had originated in Hawick Sheriff Court. It turned upon a difficult point of law upon which there was plenty of authority, both for and against. Authority is our slang for previous decisions in similiar cases. The layman thinks that every human circumstance has already been the subject of prior decision. This is not the case. The ingenuity of human affairs constantly conjures up new circumstances. It is one of the great fascinations of the law.

In the Appeal Court junior counsel for the appellant opens the case, stating his basic premises, and drawing his conclusions from them. He then presents his arguments in support of his theses. Senior counsel acts as sweeper. With his greater experience he is expected to extemporise a reply to the arguments advanced by the opposing side. I was led in my first civil case by the late James Leechman QC later Lord Leechman. When the great day came the thudding nervousness which still accompanies me into court, departed as soon as I was on my feet, and I greatly enjoyed the experience. By tradition the court does not interrupt an advocate making his maiden appearance, and this can be very off-putting. Fortunately the point in issue was sufficiently interesting for the court bit by bit to depart from tradition, and to test my argument by putting questions to me. We lost the Appeal, but I felt that I had acquitted myself well.

That case came from a solicitor who had been on the National Council of the Covenant Association. He never sent me another, but within a week, the firm acting for the other side in the Appeal had instructed me. They had an extensive practice in marine, aircraft, reparation and company law, and where they led others followed. It had taken me nearly three years, but I was off at last.

9 Trying to be Good

LIFE IS FULL of loves and hates. Happy the man who has more of the first than the second. My loves are sung frequently in these pages. My pet hate is mediocrity. It has been my enemy all my life, and although it has come to dwell with me it has never been a welcome guest. Not to fight to leave things a bit better than they were is to live like a pot-plant. To breathe, be watered, flower, fade and die is not enough for me. I do not condemn people who live like that. It may be all they can do.

But I have lived and worked among people of great talent, and the mediocrity I hate is the mediocrity of talent. West and East from Greece no country has given more to the world than Scotland. Yet the ambitious twentieth century Scot is tireless in his pursuit of the banal. Give him a house in the New Town of Edinburgh, a car, a country cottage, and a pair of status-seeking boots, and he counts himself a success. He has far more in him, but he has sold his soul. Souls have gone cheap in the twentieth century. Scotland has studied to turn aspiration into mud.

Nowhere has this been more apparent than among Scots lawyers. I could name half a dozen who could expand their abilities to fill an embassy to the United Nations. Others could take flawed arguments and rework them to speak with truth and clarity for our time and beyond. There has been wit there to confound the ugly heresy that the poor ye shall always have with you. Instead their narrow ambitions have choked them. Those who could make the Gods themselves chuckle have been content to say, 'I concur.' Foremost among such people I name James Peter Hymers MacKay, Lord MacKay of Clashfern, Lord Chancellor of England.

James and I have never been intimates, but for thirty years we have conducted a nodding acquaintance. On my side, and I think also on his, there has been an affection amounting to respect. He appointed me a sheriff. He is a very fine lawyer. He is widely read. Like me, he has firm views on the deity. Give him a principle and he can deduct it to its logical conclusions. He has a feeling for humanity. He has a warmth of personality that makes people feel better just for being in his company. His coldness of mind is that of the mathematician, not of the zealot. His vision is wide, and microscopic in detail. If he had ever been given an idea, a much rarer thing than a principle, it would have so startled him that he might have done something wonderful with it. But James has always been short of ideas. So, to be fair has the twentieth century.

James was never a politician. He was Dean of the Faculty of Advocates when conservatives were so thin on the ground that they could not even find a Lord Advocate. The bells of Bray rang for him, and he became a Tory. Then he became a Scottish judge. Then the Woolsack fell vacant and that was the end of him. Here is a man who in a week could have written a constitution for Scotland, that would have been remembered as long as the American Constitution, and might have worked better, and he is lost to us because of a petty ambition and a pretty gown. He, who could have been one of our re-founding fathers, will be remembered as a portrait on the wall, and as the executive of a few chancy reforms, designed by others. Scotland can ill spare men of James' calibre. His life has had all the direction and subtelty of a runaway Sherman tank, and it has ended up in an English bog. What has happened to us? Why do we waste our best people like this?

It is my very real respect for one of the best amongst us that makes me feel for James as I do. I come of the same stock and background. I have walked the floor of the Parliament House with him, remembering that in the Laigh Hall beneath our feet the Bluidy MacKenzie tortured his forefathers and mine for holding fast to the beliefs still held by the man who walked beside me. I have rejected those beliefs, but I admired James for holding to them. He appeared to be made of the same stuff as the Cameronians, the hard unwearing tweed-like stuff that is so much a part of our history. Then almost over-night he became a Pantaloon in silk breeches. He is lost to us.

These are the losses which bring me almost to hate our big neighbour. The attractions of the foreign panoply and array of state seem so much more glittering than our own home-spun affairs. The bended knees and the bowed backs of the flunkeys make every empty occasion seem so much more important than anything Scotland has to offer. There will be few who see Lord Clashfern's going over as anything other than a personal success. I see it as a flawed weakness in a man who could have been my friend and colleague. He was tempted, he went over, and I suspect that James found that the trumpets which sounded for him brought no satisfaction.

I too have had my temptations. In these far off days in the 1950s, just after I was called to the bar, the temptation I yielded to was to become a gentleman, a comfortable well thought of toff. Warm. Sound. Mediocre. I tried hard. I walked up and down the Mound under a monstrous bowler hat, carrying an umbrella, trying to look like the rest of the dollies, and sometimes succeeding. Yet every now and again a joyfulness of spirit broke through and I realised some of my potential. Looking back on these lost ten years it is not the progress of my career I remember with pride, but the things I did to damn and damage it irrevocably. I have failed in many things, and my proudest failure is in my attempt to be a gentleman. There is no gentility in me. I am a cad. Kenny MacKenzie started my downfall.

When you remember Lord MacKay of Clashfern, Lord Chancellor of England, remember also Kenny MacKenzie, and remember him before God, because I think he is dead now. One of life's failures, he died unknown, but not without leaving his subtle mark on our times. When I last wrote of him he was a jobbing printer in the Anderston district of Glasgow. His business failed. Its failure is no part of this story, but as I walked up the Mound I came across him again. He wore an old tattered tweed coat which bobbed around him as though he and it both carried heavy weights. They did. They carried lead slugs of poetry. Indomitable in defeat he had saved his precious linotype which he had erected in a basement in the New Town of Edinburgh, just opposite the St Vincent Church. There, alone and virtually friendless, he was setting up in type Hugh MacDiarmid's *A Drunk Man Looks at the Thistle,* and sleeping on the concrete floor beside his machine. Every now and again he loaded the pockets of his tattered coat with slugs and carried them up to Malcolm MacDonald's paper-shop in Marchmont, in the hope that somehow they would be set up, printed, and published. Hugh MacDiarmid was unknown then. It was an act of faith in a mediocre world.

Kenny and I joined forces. I scraped together some money, and Castle Wynd printers was born. In a room in Ramsay Lane, first on the right before Edinburgh Castle, we set up our printing shop. We had his linotype, and at scrap prices we bought two antique printing presses. My credit, ever a sickly companion, got us a small modern automatic platen, which somehow managed to keep itself one step ahead of the instalments, for we took in jobbing printing to keep the firm alive. For three years, while waiting for my practice to come to me, I went into the Parliament House from nine to eleven, and then to the printing shop, where work detained me into the early hours of the morning. In all we published four volumes of Hugh MacDiarmid's poetry in paperback. No one made any money. Indeed these five words make me chuckle. Money is irrelevant to poetry. In the end Castle Wynd was wound up, having made nothing and owing nothing. Kenny and I went our separate ways. I don't recall ever seeing him again. To have helped this strange lonely man to publish Christopher Murray Grieve is the proudest thing I have done with my life.

Keats says somewhere that a man's life is an allegory. If you know what that means, you are a better person than I am.

All that remains of these ten years is a mosaic. Justaposed to my increasing legal practice were incidents which had no part in the douce and perjink life of an Edinburgh lawyer. It is not really very difficult to be a success. What is much more difficult is coping with success. It's awfully dull. What was not dull was my domestic life. I begat three children, squalling puking lovely brats they were, and not one of them has become a jelly baby. I was a rotten father. I dandled and cuddled them, but not until they could give me cheek, and cut me down to size, did they become human beings to me.

Family life is very important to me, but it has never been enough. Some engrossing activity to absorb me totally when I turn from dealing with other people's affairs is also necessary. I tried writing fiction. It was so bad that even the most exciting passages sent me to sleep. I even toyed with the idea of becoming an MP, but a bonnie dearie I would look at a State Opening of Parliament. The only consolation would be to see the shamefaced and sheepish expressions worn by Donald Dewar and John Smith as they pair off with their oppos and walk into the House of Lords. They are intelligent enough to realise just how silly they look. Politics is not my thing. It means compromise, and that is difficult to achieve. I recognise our present Government because I have to, but I am in a state of treason against it. I undermine it where I can. I do not accept that we can get anything from Westminster, and certainly not Home Rule. That we create for ourselves whenever we want it. If, for a transitional year or two, we have to have representatives at Westminster, all they should be doing is creating hell, and disrupting the place, instead of bowing to the mace, that symbol of the conquest of the common people, and bowing so deeply that the beer nearly falls out. It is a beastly place, and quite alien to the Scottish character. There, they boast of their genius for compromise. In fact it is a talent to debase.

A glance at our two high officers of state show just how

debased Scottish political life has become. Malcolm Rifkind the Scottish Secretary and Peter Fraser the Lord Advocate, both Scottish silks, represent England in Scotland, not Scotland in England. Malcolm Rifkind is not the helmsman of a ship of state. He is the master of a seedy tramp loaded with a cargo of wooden horses, one of which he has left outside every Scottish political and educational institution. Peter Fraser makes a good groom. No self- respecting Scot could keep yon company for long. Westminster politics is English politics, and they are not for me. Besides, in so far as I have had a political life nine tenths of it has been spent jouking up closes to avoid Scottish Nationalists. They keep trying to convert me or execrate me. It's not clear which. My farewell to politics came through a meeting with one of them, and my coronach was a play.

While pacing up the Mound under my detested bowler it came to me that Scotland needed a radio station. Some enquiries brought home to me that money was needed to build the transmitter. John MacCormick, my dear friend and mentor, was ill, and indeed he died a year or two later. Besides he had a law-abiding streak, and private transmitters are illegal. I went to see someone else, a great Scottish Nationalist, who refused to have anything to do with the scheme. Then he produced a whisky bottle, and started to sing. He sang a lot, and one of his songs went something like this.

> Oh sound the pibroch loud and high,
> From John O'Groats to Isle of Skye.
> Oh up your pipe and fo and fi.
> We'll fight and die for Chairlie.

The chorus is even better.

> Hutchin fo-am fo-am
> Hutchin fo-am fo-am
> Hutchin fo-am fo-am
> We'll fight and die for Chairlie

108

I went home in a fury and wrote a play.

The Tinkers of the World is a tragedy in which I created a busy thriving island community, and then introduced the man from the Ministry, who announced that the island was to be taken over and the people resettled on the mainland with massive resettlement grants. Then the island was to be used as a rocket bomb testing range, 'in the interests of us all'. The principal character, a wee Glasgow nyaff, I named Roddy. I already had in mind the actor I wanted to play the part. I had seen him play a small part in the film of Eric Linklater's book *Laxdale Hall*. He was Roddy MacMillan. Roddy was later to make his name both as an actor on stage and television, but particularly, to my mind, as a playwright. His plays *All in Good Faith* and *The Bevellers* deserve constant revival. In my play he was the small feckless betrayed man, helpless in the grip of vast forces. Predictably he, and the cheif's English educated daughter were the only two who fought to the end, but hopelessly, as the natural leaders of the people fell off one by one, leaving them alone.

The Tinkers opened at the Gateway Theatre in Leith Walk in February 1957 for a fortnight. It was produced and directed by Lennox Milne, wife of Moray MacLaren whose books have always delighted me, and whose friendship delighted me even more. Roddy MacMillan was great. My only complaint was about the audience. Most of Roddy's lines were in Scots, specifically in the Paisley version of the Scots I had been rebuked for speaking as a child. Interestingly linguistically, Roddy asked me to change 'Ken' to 'know' in his lines as 'know' came more naturally to him. 'Ken' is Norse and 'know' is Middle English, and in Paisley we say the one, in Glasgow the other. People in Edinburgh laugh at anything with a Scots accent, and this angered me. I had to rebuke some of the lesser actors in some of the later performances for playing the lines for cheap laughs.

By and large the play worked. The critics liked it, one of them even comparing it to, 'the Sean O'casey of the earlier plays'. The final lines, spoken by the Chief's daughter, contained the agony I have felt for Scotland then and since.

> *We are the broken clans. We are the tinkers of*
> *the world. We are the Americans and the Canadians*
> *and the Australians but we are no longer the*
> *dwellers in our own places. We have been cast*
> *out and we have not lifted a hand to defend*
> *ourselves. Why are we scattered like this? Is*
> *there nothing left that my people think is worth*
> *fighting and dying for?*

As the curtain falls her drunken father sings off-stage,

> *Hutchin fo-am fo-am fo-am*
> *We'll fight and die for Chairlie.*

The Tinkers had another fine production on steam radio. It was produced by Finlay J. MacDonald with Roddy in the lead, Norman Shelley as the chief, and that fine actress Annette Crosbie as the chief's daughter. I liked the radio production. It went out live, and I sat in the control box as it was broadcast but it wasn't as exciting as a first night. Seeing your own characters come alive on the stage is something wonderful.

There was a sequel. At that time the Foyle family was trying to encourage the professional repertory theatre in Britain. The Foyle Award, a cheque for the playwright and a plaque for the theatre, was given annually to the play adjudged to be the best new play produced in any repertory theatre in Britain. It was much sought after and had come to Scotland only once before for Moray MacLaren's *One Traveller Returns*. *The Tinkers* won the award for 1957, and it was presented to me in London, the first time I had been back there since the Stone of Destiny.

The Tinkers satirised latter day Jacobitism, and it helped me to slough off any personal political ambitions I had ever had. I am not geared up to humbug. I should have liked instead to be a playwright, but although I kept hard at my typewriter, nothing I wrote thereafter was worth a tosser. Yet seeing my characters on the stage let me have a chance to have a look at myself, and I knew that I was not cut out for anything except the humdrum drudgery of earning a living. Still, while preserving the surface demeanour of a staid advocate, some levity managed to creep into my spirit. Out of court I cannot be solemn for very long, and I get into trouble. Jacobitism and my attitude to it led to the expulsion of Christopher Grieve and myself from the Heather Club of Edinburgh.

The Heather Club is an ancient institution, or so they say. It is supposed to have started as a dining-club among those Jacobites who had, 'taken to the heather'. It held, and I suppose still holds an annual dinner to which 'The Captain' invites a guest to give 'The Oration'. It's better than Burns. Christopher Grieve was to give the oration that night, and as I was to give it the following year I was asked along also. The Captain was a solicitor who sent me work from time to time, although he never did again after that night. Ever one for a free dinner I took Sheila along with me.

While we ate a lady sang songs about a wee burn wimpling in the bottom of the glen and a bonnie briar bush, and I was pretty sick about it all. I was not at the top table but as I was to be guest of honour the following year life membership of the club was bestowed upon me along with Christopher. Christopher had as usual prepared his speech, and he read it to a rude and unappreciative audience who talked to one another throughout. They had expected something more rousing. Such engagements were unpaid, and indeed Christopher had paid his own expenses to come in from the country to entertain these Philistines. He was their guest in every sense of the word. He sat down to a scattering of applause and drank two large whiskies. Speaking was an ordeal to him. I could see that he was not pleased. Neither was I. Then we had another song.

That night there had been a report and a photograph in the

Edinburgh *Evening News* of the gable wall of an Edinburgh tenement falling down from neglect, and exposing the pitiful houses of the very poor. In my mind it was a bitter contrast to these sleekit Jacobites, when suddenly the wailing of the singer stopped, and to my horror I heard my name being called by the chairman. Without any warning or prior arrangement he called upon me to speak. It was quite unforgivable. I rose and spoke.

'Tonight,' I said, 'two things have happened which do not concern you. A tenement building has fallen down leaving people homeless, and you sing of a wee burn wimpling at the bottom of a glen. The second is that you have insulted your guest, the greatest of living Scotsmen, by your very presence in the same room as him.' If you are going to insult a roomful of people, do it roundly.

I continued in the same vein, pausing now and again for applause. Since I was using my loud orator's voice people began to applaud the sound before they grasped the content. The first to realise what I was saying was a Bailie who thought that I was condemning the City's housing programme. He called out that his party's housing record was second to none. Because the entertainment had been mawkish, their treatment of their guest shameful, and this being Scotland, some people agreed with me. There were cheers as well as cries of outrage. When I sat down Christopher rose again and restarted where I had left off. The Heather Club now got their rousing oration, and they did not like it.

'Ian Hamilton is quite right,' the great old lion roared, getting on to the only topic he knew when he was angered. 'You can never trust the English, and I am among the English tonight.'

The audience listened to him in awed silence. Finally he reached his coda. Then the Captain called desperately on the pianist to play something for God's sake, and the pianist, moved by the impetus of great events, obliged with Scots Wha

Hae. I stood to attention, Christopher stood to attention, and the dinner broke up in disorder. They took us by the shoulder and put us out in the street, the Bailie shouting wrathfully after us 'Youse are expelled'.

As the years rolled on I managed with considerable difficulty to keep out of further trouble. One night it was only by a hair's breadth. The advocates' robing-room is sometimes an entertaining place, and one day we were discussing the possibilities of a criminal disguising himself so cleverly that not even his own friends could recognise him. The general consensus was that it was impossible. A friend who ornaments the sherival bench was particularly adamant.

'Can't be done, Hamilton. Never. Quite beyond my experience. Impossible.'

He was a great conversation stopper, was Sheriff Horatio. I was not so sure. Maybe his experience did not go that far. Besides his complacency was a trifle jarring. Maybe he was suffering from that hardening of the spirit, if not of the arteries, which sometimes afflicts sheriffs. A bold and practical contradiction would be a favour to him. But what disguise?

To be successful a disguise must do many things. It must shield the eyes, because a glance betrays you. It has to change your gait, because your gait is significant. It must conceal also your voice. That would immediately give you away. And of course it must disguise all your features. I reckoned that a Greek Orthodox priest might just do the trick. It was Festival time, and Horatio was not a festive character. He was wont of an evening to sit staring gloomily into a glass in one of several hostelries. He would be easily found.

One evening I went down to the Gateway Theatre, and explained my problem to Sadie Aitken, the manageress. Sadie was a great character. She dressed in black bombazine and was very C of S very staid, or so she looked. We had always got on like a house on fire, and since she thought they had screwed me on my contract with *The Tinkers* she was always slipping

113

me free tickets. A costume for a Greek Orthodox priest was nothing to her, and she soon raked one out of the wardrobe. The cast of the show gathered round me, watched me dress, and made me up with eager cries of encouragement.

At their hands a terrifying change came over me. My face, my young face, became old and lined, and most of it was covered with a long straggling dirty greyish beard stuck on with glue. Another person looked out the mirror at me, and when a pair of pebble glasses covered my eyes life became a daze. A giant's cut-down dinner suit trousers, with the hem at my hips and the crotch at my knees changed my gait and a frock-coat, a beretta and an unfurled umbrella completed the outfit. We Greek Orthodox priests never furl our umbrellas. Just before I stepped out into the street Sadie put a great glass ring on my finger, and made me a bishop.

It is a strange sensation going out onto the street as another person. At first you want to bolt back, but when I tried, the stage door was locked on me, and behind it I could hear the uncontrolled laughter of the Gateway cast. There was nothing for it but to stride out stumping my umbrella on the pavement. Then a strange thing happened. No one took any notice of me. I was a Greek Orthodox priest.

I popped into the Windsor Bar where there were people I knew. Not one paid any attention, except to make way for me.

'Shenny', I said, pointing at the gantry impatiently. 'Shenny'.

'Try the old bastard with gin,' said one of the drinkers, and gin it was. Then I set out round the pubs looking for Horatio.

Many pubs later I found him sitting at the bar of the Scotia Hotel in Great King Street. I slipped on to a stool beside him.

' Well, Horatio. What'll you have to drink?'

'Jesus Christ,' said the sheriff, and shot out the door.

I heard later that the fright sent him T T for a week.

After that a certain hazy carelessness set in. Princes Street called me and there I waved my umbrella at a taxi to take my conquests further. A kindly Irishman came to help me and just before I got into the taxi I so far forgot myself as to hold out my hamd to him and say, 'Thank you, Paddy.' Reverently he bent to kiss the ring, and then my accent penetrated to him. He was very properly and rightly outraged. He seized out a great fistful of my beard, ever a painful happening, and started to shout for the police. This gave me a moment and I dodged among the traffic and across Princes Street. I hitched up the trousers, disclosing my legs to the knees, and pelted up Frederick Street, and hid in a close until the shouting died down. Then I went home. Never, never again did I dress up like that. It could be misconstrued as a breach of the peace.

Circumstances are always more monstrous in reality. Next day my practice took me to Glasgow. The Glasgow train bides at Queen Street station Glasgow for only a few moments before it shuttles back to Edinburgh. As I got off the train a Greek Orthodox priest, my spitten image of the night before, got onto it Edinburgh bound. Next day I searched the papers with fearful glee to see if he had met up with the outraged Irishman, but I don't think he did.

After that incident life became once more prosaic and my legal practice grew apace. A general election returned Labour to be the Party of Government. I was not a member of the Labour Party, and at that time all the Lord Advocate's Deputes were considered to be members of the Government, and fell when the Government fell. Gordon Stott, who had ever a kind word for me became Lord Advocate, and did me the honour of asking me to join his team. I did. To become an advocate depute is the first public badge and recognition of success.

Paradoxically, but not perhaps surprisingly, Sheila now got fed up with my antics, and she asked me to leave the family home. I took a cottage in the country not far from Edinburgh, never to resume living with her. I was shattered. For the first year or two I could not believe that it was permanent, and I continued to live day by day, which is the only way to live when your breath has been taken from you.

10 African Interlude

THE LOSS OF SHEILA was the loss of all the world to me and the world was well lost for the years I had with her. I did not seek street corner access to the children. They had to find their lives without me. The family circle had narrowed to exclude me, but it was still the family circle. There was no place for an intruding father. This is not the conventional view, but it is mine. Far too many estranged parents fight one another over the weeping bodies of their children. Long after, but not until they were in their teens, the three of them came back to me. One after the other, tentatively at first, they sought me out and found they liked me, and we have become a family once again. But yon was a grim time.

An advocate depute in those days normally held office for two years, but after fifteen months the strain of hoping to meet my children round each street corner began to prey on me, and a new departure was needed. Zambia, the old Northern Rhodesia, had just obtained independence. Kenneth Kaunda its President had been educated in a Scottish mission school, and he wanted a Scottish advocate to set up a department of civil litigation. I put my name forward and in December 1966 I flew out to Zambia's perpetual summer, hoping the change would alter my whole life. It did nothing of the kind. Latin tags can be silly and pretentious, but two lines of Horace have a wisdom which sums up my position then. In my personal wilderness in Zambia they haunted me. *Quis patriae exul se quoque fugit?* asks one line. Elsewhere Horace answers his own question. *Coulum non animum mutant qui trans mari fugant.* Translated these lines mean, What man exiled from his country, escapes also from himself? The answer is simple. People who run away do not change themselves. They only change the skies above. I accompanied myself to Zambia.

Zambia was as good a place as any and better than most to

nurse my loneliness. The sun always shone. After the ancient soft blended colours of Scotland the red red soil and the flaming trees assaulted the eye. Soil redder than the soil of the Mearns is the abiding impression. There is little perspective of distance as the bush, grey rather than green, rolls on for ever and can only be seen from the air. There are few vantage points to overlook the country, and none from the capital, Lusaka. The climate is never too hot because the great central plain of Africa is at nearly five thousand feet, and on a June winter's morning there is frost on the ground. In October the humidity builds up and so do human tensions. Murder month it is called because the murder rate soars as the human body like all the earth strains for rain. On 5 November the rains come, great desalinating warm rains which soak you between the kerb and the porch, and what a relief it is. Yet the abiding noise of Zambia is not water but the chorus of millions of evening cicadas.

The Zambian has many of the attributes of the Scotsman. He laughs at weddings, marvels at birth, and grieves at death. He has never adopted the silly English habit of drinking in moderation. He loves a bevvy. Perhaps he has more laughter than we have because he does not need to work so hard. In Zambia in my time the soil was plentiful and fertile. In a few weeks mealies, that is maize, grew to ripeness. From mealies comes the staple diet, and from it also comes chibuko the African beer, a sort of fermented porridge. The diet is woefully short of protein but even in the people from the far bush there was little sign of malnutrition. There was plenty of other disease, God knows, but I have seen more malnutrition in Glasgow than was apparent in the illiterate bush people. Illiteracy is a term of abuse to us ignorant Europeans. Little more than a hundred years ago most of the English were illiterate. Being illiterate the African sings and laughs at his work and appearing happy makes those round about him happy. At least that is my impression. I was only there for fifteen months.

117

Geoffrey Pimm, the Senior State Advocate met me at Lusaka. He became a good friend and like many good friends there was much about him I did not know and never learned. His friendship stood always behind me and never wavered. He is now back in practice at the English Bar and he sent me a kind note many years later when I took silk. What took him to Zambia was a mystery. Many of my non-African colleagues would have been pushed to earn as good a living in Britain, but he was not like that. I thought I was friendless in Africa, but unknowingly I made many friends who have endured over the years. Geoffrey has been one of them.

Geoffrey took me to the Ministry of Justice and introduced me to Billy Menari, an Ulsterman who was Solicitor General. He was small, intense, eager, non-political, dark, and utterly pragmatic. He held no other idea than faithfully to serve out his time and get on to something else, perhaps just death. He was my boss, and apart from the fact that I cannot work for a boss we got on fine. At our first meeting he asked me if I would like to be a parliamentary draftsman. This took me aback. Parliamentary draftsmen are the scum of the profession. They take the turgid thoughts of politicians and turn them into Acts of Parliament. They are the only people who can give three different meanings, each one contradictory, to the already obscure. Billy Menari listened to these truths with politeness. Then he informed me that in Zambia the Solicitor General was the head Parliamentary draftsman.

Apart from drafting, the only other work in the Ministry of Justice visible to my eyes was the prosecution of crime. It was assumed that I knew nothing about that. Having damned myself utterly from the cream of the work, as drafting was regarded, my way was clear to get down to civil litigation. I now know, or at least have guessed, that the decision to have a Department of Civil Litigation was a political one, taken either at high civil service or cabinet level. Having resolved it into existence no one had any interest in it producing anything. The resolution had been implemented, and my presence was the proof of it. To be in charge of a Department of Civil Litigation seems very grand. It was nothing of the kind. Moreover I had thought that I was going there in a consultant capacity. This was not the case. It was a civil service job. So long as I turned up at 8 am and left at 4 pm each as mandatory as the other, I could have sat out my whole three-year term in my little office throwing peanut shells at the wall and notching up my gratuity. I very nearly did. Getting a key to the Ministry building was a major operation, and given as a major concession. No one had ever returned in the evening to get on with their work.

When asked for work Billy Menari washed his hands of me and gave me the Zambian constitution to read. I had nothing to do day after day but read the constitution. I kept asking for work, and was promised it but none came. It was like my early years at the Bar. I was again a briefless advocate. Then someone from some Ministry got lost one day and came to me by mistake. Word got round the Ministries and people began to send their problems.

Somehow and from hidden places where they had long reposed I dug out files of cases where people owed money some of which had been outstanding since before independence. Recovering some of that money became one of my jobs. I could have recovered several million, some of it in hard currency, had I had any staff, but none could be spared. The draftsmen had them all. When I got a typewriter and did my own typing a memo was sent round forbidding this practice. It was derogatory to the dignity of senior civil servants. Yet I managed to collect quite a few of the debts outstanding to the Government, and as soon as I did so I ran into trouble.

Two principles should guide a lawyer when he handles money. The first is to give a receipt for it, and the second is to get rid of it as soon as possible. If he cannot get rid of it he can at least lay it out at interest. When I began to take in money no one knew what to do with it. Other than a receipt-book which I had bought in down town Lusaka, and a memo in my own diary there was no accounting procedure to deal with it. I could have put it in my pocket because large sums were paid to me alone in my tiny room in cash. Since it belonged to no one's 'vote' it was a sort of bastard child. If there is one thing worse in the civil service than embezzling money, it is producing it. It creates a problem that no one can solve.

The simple and obvious solution got me into terrible trouble. They told me to put the money in the office safe which was no solution. Some of the money was in cheques even if quite a lot was in cash. Cheques should be presented as soon as possible and large sums in cash should not be kept in an office safe. I went down town and opened an account in a building society in the name of the Government of the Republic of Zambia. The thin peevish wailing of civil servants at this action had to be heard to be believed. The Treasury were incensed. Only the Treasury could open a Government bank account, they said, and were not consoled when it was pointed that their premise was obviously false as I had just opened one. Treasury civil servants the world over seem to think themselves a higher order of creation. The rumblings were still going on when I left Zambia many months later. The problem went unsolved, and I was directed to stop taking in any further money until due accounting procedures could be created. Don't pay me. I'm too poor to buy a purse. That was the system the poor Zambians inherited from our civil service.

The civil service looks after itself. The flat which went with the job was a very comfortable one in a civil service cantonment. It was lonely of course, but that had been brought in with my baggage. One evening a dog followed me home from the airport bar where I had been drinking. People are like that. They go away and leave their dogs. The two great dogs in my life have been strays. Braan was abandoned in Glen Lochy in Argyll, and Friday, as I called him, at Lusaka airport. I have never quite got over either of them.

Friday was some sort of Scotch collie cross. Long before I got him he had been hit by a car and he had a shattered left shoulder, and a withered left foreleg. I took him to the vet to have him put down. The vet, a kindly Swede with the Scottish name of Neilson, said he was in no pain. Since he got along on three legs as well as others did on four I kept him and we became a great comfort to each other. Shortly after we met he became ill with biliary fever and grew so weak that he could scarcely follow me. He was given injections and it was touch and go for several days. He could not walk or drink and I had to squeeze water into his mouth with cotton wool. I carried him with me to the Ministry which was strictly against the rules, but I would have killed anyone who interfered and nobody did. Gradually he got better and after that the bond between us was closer still. Deverilius, who looked after me said that out of the fifty or more cars which drove to the flats at day's end, Friday always knew the sound of mine.

You were supposed to keep a dog on a lead in downtown Lusaka because of the danger of rabies. Friday did not need one. The more crowded the street, the more he tapped his nose on the back of my left leg to let me know he was still there. If anyone said anything I took off my tie and used it as a lead. If I was in undress I had a tie holding up my trousers. He came to court with me and lay on my jacket in the robing room until the court rose. He had no interest in anyone else and he did not have a vicious streak in him. He even became an honorary member of a Royal Air Force Officers' Mess.

There was a Royal Air Force presence in Zambia because Ian Smith had just declared unilateral independence in the neighbouring state of Southern Rhodesia. Many of the pilots and navigators became my friends, and Friday became a favourite with them. Having regard to my earlier expressed views on peacetime soldiers I can only say that inconsistency is a rare virtue. Some of these fellows are still my friends. We lived a pretty wild life, but not so wild that it has anything to do with this story. I did some entertaining, but more with a glass than a knife-and-fork as you need a woman to preside over a table.

My table was looked after by Deverilius Piri. He was my houseboy. The term is a patronising one, although he would not have thought so. We became friends and he looked after me with great kindness. Simple people are like that. The two people who have looked after me without stint were both simple people. They were Deverilius and Christine MacRitchie, our Edinburgh house-keeper. Paying Deverilius was the difficulty. To pay him adequately would 'spoil him' as the saying went. An adequate wage in my eyes would have been outrageous wealth by African standards. I salved my conscience by buying him such things as a bicycle, which was an object of great wealth to him. I also gave him blankets and other domestic items. He had to get a chit with them, as even in self-governing Zambia possession of such 'European' articles would have raised a presumption of theft.

Deverilius belonged to the Nanja tribe, and the Bemba were in the ascendant. He could read and write both English and Nanja, and this was a considerable educational achievement. It was more than I could do. Since he was of the wrong tribe he had no chance of ever getting a job in the civil service. That was the province of the Bemba, and very able people they were. The African is determined to be master in his own country. Simple as that observation may be it is not an easy one for a white man to accept. Oppression flaws the oppressor as much as it hurts the oppressed. The assumption that the white man can do things better is not an easy one for him to give up. Transition from white rule to black rule went smoothly while I was in Zambia, and there was little crime even in a large city like Lusaka.

Lusaka is a modern city and in those days one could walk

its streets in safety. We were supposed to take all our recreation in town or somewhere up or down the line of road and rail, which stretches north and south through the country. It is part of the vanished Victorian dream of the Cape-to-Cairo railway. All round was the bush. We were not encouraged to go into it, and you could easily get lost. I always carried a compass, but it was dull country for walking in. I only once came across a village and there they shyly treated me as an honoured guest and gave me chibuko to drink. It was served in a tin that a long time previously had contained a pint of Mobile Oil. In that village that tin was wealth. We drank sitting on the beaten ground of the village in front of the mud and thatch huts. A few patches for mealies had been hewn out of the bush, which surrounded us in all directions. Beyond the men's circle the children sucked their fingers in awe, their eyes rolling white in their velvety skins, and the lovely dark women giggled in the further background. They were very very lovely indeed. I could happily have gone native with any one of them.

I doubt if there were many wild animals in the bush around Lusaka, but we sometimes saw baboons, which can be very dangerous indeed. When they attack in a pack they go into a sort of frenzy. There were certainly snakes and when I caught one and sent it home it caused consternation in Edinburgh. An acquaintance asked me to go out to his house to shoot a snake which had taken up residence in his aviary and was eating his budgies. From his description of it, it seemed to be a cobra, probably a black spitting cobra, and this proved to be correct. I went dressed in borrowed riding boots and riding breeches, and wore flying goggles. A friend who was a nurse stood by with a hypodermic of Fitzimmons snake-bite serum. The snake was hiding under a small hut, and when this was overturned it revealed itself in all its shiny black coiled nastiness. It was about four feet long, and it reared and struck. You distract it with a handkerchief, and when it is striking at that you catch it

123

firmly in the circle of your finger and thumb, just behind the head. That's what the book says, and that is how I did it. Cobras are slower than men, but it had time to spit several lines of venom across my goggles.

Snakes go into a coma when put into a bag, and a pillowslip did fine. Packaged in the approved air freight fashion it was further protected by being put into a cardboard box that had contained Heinz beans. A telephone call to Edinburgh Zoo, warned them of its arrival but the line was bad and Gilbert Fisher the curator did not know that I was in Africa and thought that it was a joke. He should have known better. An advocate founded Edinburgh Zoo. Gilbert was not at the airport to meet the cobra when it arrived. International airports are used to such packages but internal ones are not. When a Heinz bean box marked VENOMOUS REPTILE in large red letters arrived at Edinburgh the cargo handlers went on strike and the aircraft was taxied to a far corner of the tarmac by a very reluctant pilot. Gilbert Fisher was summoned from his bed to sort the matter out, which he told me later he did very gingerly indeed. People have said that it was rash to catch the cobra. It wasn't. All the approved precautions were taken, and the same people who say it was rash, probably run downstairs with their hands in their pockets, which is a much more dangerous thing to do.

The cobra lived for many years in the zoo, and the kids saw it. It thrilled them to see the 'Presented by' tag outside the cage. Zoos are for kids and for people without imagination. Sending the snake there was marginally better than taking a twelve bore to it, but I would rather be shot. However, catching it was a welcome break from the routine work of a civil servant.

The civil work was never sufficient to keep me going full time, particularly as there was no staff for my department. There was however always a lack of prosecutors, and to plug a gap they sent me into the criminal courts. No duck greeted water with a louder quack. They hanged murderers and I frequently found myself with capital charges on my hands. It would be easy to strike an attitude and say how repugnant it all was, but it is no worse than prosecuting people to rot in Victorian jails, which were never designed for long term prisoners. I prosecuted fairly, and some people hanged. I am as surely a killer as anyone who has pointed a gun at a fellow human and pulled a trigger. The only difference is that I was licensed to kill. Hanging deters nobody, and most murder is more tragic than wicked. Crime was much the same in Zambia as in Scotland, except that African society has higher moral standards in its view of property. There is less greed. As for procedure, except that everything is done through an interpreter and there is no jury, the trials in Zambia were very much the same as at home.

People were brought in from the far bush for these trials and they squatted with endless patience in the corridors of the High Court. Everyone has their smell, and the African's smell is different from ours. Were I ever to smell it again, it would take me back to questioning these calm dignified people. When asked the time that some event had taken place the witness would silently indicate with outstretched arm the distance the sun had risen above the horizon. If it was the afternoon, he would turn his back and give the same salute to a setting sun. Try reading the Scriptures again, remembering that they were written about a people without clocks. Christ would indicate the hour to his disciples in the same way.

People often ask me about seeing game and the answer is that apart from elephant seen from a boat on Lake Kariba, and hippo in the Kafue river I saw none at all. The elephants were at a distance, and if you have seen Ailsa Craig a hippopotamus is a disappointment. I managed two long distance trips by road, but neither in Scotland nor in Africa can you expect to see much from a road.

On the first trip my thumb got me a lift on a lorry going to Isoka on the Tanzanian frontier. The road was a single track dirt road and the lorry was going there to pick up drums of petrol. The round trip was about a thousand miles. I forget how many days it took but I overstayed my leave and was frowned upon on my return. We had to sleep under the lorry on that trip, the two African drivers and myself, as they said we were in leopard country. Leopards won't crawl under lorries, or so they said. As there was no room in the cab for sleeping I took their word for it. Although frowned at by officialdom these trips were more than a personal adventure. I was responsible for the Government's road traffic insurance, and I sat on a board which apportioned blame for damage to Zambian Government vehicles. I felt that it was necessary to know something more than conditions in downtown Lusaka.

The other trip I managed was in my own Fiat 500, which I drove from Lusaka to Fort Jameson, 400 miles east on the Malawi frontier. The necessary supplies of petrol food and water for the journey overloaded the tiny car. The trip took two days each way along a dirt road which had been corrugated by a grader. It was of no interest to anyone but myself. The bush is featureless; scrub growth alternates with tall trees and open parkland. The red dusty road goes on for ever. No human habitation or other sign of man exists other than the road itself. I never saw another vehicle in the whole eight hundred miles of the round trip. When the carburettor of my tiny car got choked with dust I had to dismantle it and wash it out. There was a twelve bore under my bed roll on the back seat which I carried on the insistence of some old African hands. They said there was a slight risk of being charged by elephant or rhino. According to them you knelt and waited until the beast was so close you could see the size of its eye, and then you gave it both barrels in the foremost knee, which brought it tumbling down, and you had then time to re-load and kill it. Maybe they were having me on but I was taking no chances. I never met any elephant or rhino.

I had a more poignant meeting. At one point a small cairn

on a little eminence above the road caught my eye, and I stopped to investigate. Apart from the rest house it was the only sign of a human hand between Lusaka and Fort Jameson. Only someone who has driven along a bush road can appreciate how rare such a thing can be. A Scots cairn far in the African bush. When I climbed up I found a bronze plate and on it the words, 'Near this spot David Livingstone, the Scottish traveller, first caught sight of the Luangwa river'. I stood there with a ghost's hand on my shoulder, all that long way from our homes.

No one could tell me who had erected the cairn or who had purchased the plaque. That it still stood there was also a mystery. The plaque would be a thing of value to an African either as a totem or to cut into an artifact. Perhaps the name of Livingstone surrounded the place with some juju. He is a man much venerated in Africa, where he is known as Munali, the red man, after his countenance. Whites are the only people who think they are white. Many African schools are named Munali after this strange man. If you read his diaries you find that more than the Bible took him to Africa. He had the Scots curse of wanting to see beyond far horizons.

I had tried to serve my employers well, and in many ways I believe I did so. The only capital asset a lawyer has is his integrity and that was always at their disposal. For that reason, and for many others I did not make a good civil servant. Such a person's job is to serve without question, and to carry out the will of his masters, whatever their will may be. But an independent Scots lawyer, is trained to advise, not to do what he is told, and on occasions too numerous to relate I had fallen out with my employers over the simple interpretation of where my duties lay. Neither of us was trying to outdo the other. I was as independent of the Republic of Zambia, as the Republic of Zambia was independent of me. On that fundamental difference we finally parted.

When the British left the old Northern Rhodesia they left a

constitution, all nicely modelled on Westminster, where everyone is a jolly good fellow. The British were filled with good intentions towards their former colonial subjects, but the Zambians had other ideas. It was now their avowed intention to turn the country into a one party state. U N I P The United National Independence Party was in power, and drew its support from the Bemba, 'the faithful Bemba' who carried David Livingstone's body to the coast as his tomb in Westminster Abbey narrates. To fall out with U N I P was not wise. Colin Cunningham fell out with them very much to his cost, and I got caught up in his troubles, not from any desire on my part but as surely as water runs down hill.

Colin Cunningham was one of my brother lawyers, but in private practice, and a true advocate he was. He had an English accent but all the instincts of his Scottish name. He was in his thirties or forties then, tall, somewhat angular in looks, and arrogant and domineering of manner. We fought one another from the day we met. At first I was not sure that I liked him, but I admired him as an able pleader. Later, in amity we sometimes had a drink together after court, and I admired him even more. He was a straightforward honest man. Before independence he had outraged the British civil administration by invoking every law in the book in support of the African nationalists. The old Colonial Government feared and loathed him. To the Africans he was a hero. Then independence came and he was offered his reward. He turned down the office of Chief Justice of Zambia, saying that there were troubled times ahead, and doubtless there would be much need of a good defence lawyer. Such an attitude enrages any establishment, and the Zambian establishment was no exception.

Colin Cunningham was a successful man. He had a fine house and a fine library which was later confiscated to become part of the Zambian University library. He had much to lose yet he never swerved from his duty to our profession. I had only a job to lose, he his all. He had a big civil practice, yet as long as Colin was in practice no poor man on a serious charge ever went without an advocate, however unpopular his cause.

At the time in question a small businessman running a butcher's shop was fighting it out with the Municipality, who were of course U N I P in one of their many guises. He had supplied a frozen turkey to the wife of a Government Minister who had ordered a frozen chicken. Not being familiar with the taste of turkey the Minister and his wife believed that they had been given a chicken which had 'gone off'. I need not go into all the details, but the matter got quite out of hand, and the Municipality, as municipalties will try to do anywhere, tried to close him down. Colin Cunningham was acting for the butcher.

They had just succeeded in one of their actions against the Municipality when the U N I P youth descended on his shop, smashing it up completely. He escaped out the back door and was only saved from death by hiding in the block of flats where I lived. U N I P youth were not boy scouts, but organised young men who were driven about in crowded lorries, shouting the national slogan of, 'One Zambia. One Nation'. It came across like Seig heil.

The matter went on with much fear and violence. The Mayor of Lusaka announced that U N I P ruled and not the courts, and was sentenced for contempt, a sentence which the President quashed, no doubt with reluctance, and in the hope of preserving order. I do not know how the matter ended for the butcher, but for me and Colin it ended in the course of a murder trial which I was prosecuting. Rumours abounded that morning, and when I got to court I found Colin, who was no coward, white-faced and anxious. He had had his house and office raided in the early hours of the morning. All his files had been taken away by the police, who had acted illegally and without warrant. You may ask why? I cannot answer, except to say that it could happen here, and often does. It is one of my jobs to fight the wrongful exercise of police powers.

Such a circumstance is a crisis for any lawyer whichever side of the Bar he is on. I could have minded my own business and let the matter blow by me. Colin did not expect me to do anything, and it might have been wiser to do and say nothing. Yet the Government who had carried out this illegal act were my employers, and I would have been lending the presence and comfort of a Scottish advocate to their action if I had remained silent. Colin certainly thanked me for what I did, and told me I was the only consolation to him in the whole sorry business.

A judge has few powers outside the narrow confines of the case before him, yet even in Zambia his court is an open court and what is said is noted in the record of the proceedings and ultimately internationally. Accordingly when my case was called that morning I drew the attention of the Bench to the fact that the repositories of a fellow lawyer had been searched without warrant and his papers seized by the police. Such an action, I said, affected the right of every lawyer to appear in Court without let or hindrance. My statement was received in silence. Ten minutes later I felt a tug on my gown and I was summoned to the presence of the Solicitor General. I left my junior to take over the case, never to return. The Solicitor General gave me the opportunity to resign, which I refused, and he then ordered me to leave the country by the first aeroplane which was in three days time.

For these three days I had to go into hiding. I was advised to do so by old Africa hands and I took the advice. I am a coward when there is any chance of personal violence, and they seemed to think that I might be treated as the little butcher had nearly been treated. An English Roman Catholic family hid me at the behest of an Irishman with whom I had been in the habit of playing chess. I mention their religion as I have ever found the Roman Church, and the Free Presbyterians to be the least afraid of the state. A great crowd of people turned up at the airport to see me off, among whom was Colin Cunningham.

They came to see me safely on to the aeroplane. It was an act of courage for Colin to appear at the airport. He was a marked man. A few days after I left someone tipped him some information and he made the frontier just before news of the warrant for his arrest reached it. I do not know what he was to be charged with. It had nothing to do with politics. He was just an honest lawyer. He lost everything. The last I heard of him he was teaching in Zimbabwe.

I lost my job and my dog. There was no time and indeed no facility to have him shipped back to quarantine in this country. I did the best I could for him and left him with friends.

11 Police – Servants or Masters

IT WAS NO DISGRACE to be thrown out of Zambia. Perhaps I had done wrong by my employers, but I do not think so. The unrest went on, and within a year the Attorney General who had signed my deportation papers and the Chief Justice of Zambia had to hide in a cupboard in the High Court while a mob looted the building and searched for them to lynch them. They too were ushered out of the country.

My loss was intangible. I had loved the Africans. Their enormous zest for life, and their singing and laughter as they went about their ordinary tasks, called to my Celtic blood. Except for the politics of the situation I could have gone on working there for a year or two, but always missing Scotland. Some day Zambia will settle down and be a fine country to live in, but it was not then for me. My cursed Presbyterian conscience made it difficult for me to keep my mouth shut, and anyway the atmosphere and ethos of a civil service job is not quite my cup of tea.

I had scarcely the price of a cup of tea when I arrived back in Edinburgh. My gratuity was forfeited by my sacking, and I had got out with only a bundle of clothes wrapped in a sleeping bag. My only asset was the remnants of my salary in a bank in Lusaka, and the Zambian exchange control regulations forbade me getting it out of the country. On my bank manager's advice I drew a cheque on the Zambian bank for the full amount and to the surprise of both of us the money came through. That gave me a little, but it was a very little. There were times when I went hungry, really hungry, and I was too proud to borrow from my friends, who did not know my true state. If you have been a helper all your life you do not know how to cope with needing help. Accepting help is infinitely more difficult than giving it.

No help would have done anything for my state of mind so

far as my family was concerned. Since then I have been able to help people who are going through the same experience. The bereaved always blames himself, whether the bereavement comes from death or divorce. Always you think of what you might have done differently, and wish you had. You become paranoid. You brood. I found that I could not talk about it to anyone. Now that I have helped others by listening to their troubles, I know how much it helps just to be listened to. The worst thing was knowing how to deal with my children, but I persevered in keeping away from them. I wanted desperately to see them, but not at any price. Anyone can deal with being down-and-out broke, but to be down-and-out emotionally at the same time is one of life's worst experiences. Casual friends came to my rescue. Hugh and Milicent Sims took me in, and they and their family and their near-adopted son Larry Nesbit, now a senior member of the Junior Bar, looked after me at a time when I could scarcely look after myself. Bit by bit I came to, but the way of a dissenter is hard, and there have been many times throughout my life when I have needed every friend I have. My return from Zambia was about the worst so far.

As I recovered my self-confidence, so also I recovered my ability to work. Gordon Stott, still the Lord Advocate, had confidence in me, and he put me to work as a temporary sheriff, sitting in various Sheriff Courts throughout Scotland until my practice began to return. I acquired an old banger of a car and Larry Nesbit, who at that time was a student, often came with me and sat in my court listening to the day's business, which was almost invariably the trial of petty crime.

My old banger was not the type of car which sheriffs usually drove, and the anorak, and woolly hat I now wear in winter is not advocate's formal dress. This led to a brush with a pompous and bullying police sergeant. I was sitting as interim sheriff in Hamilton and I drove into the car park and into the space marked 'SHERIFF'. The police sergeant, quick off his mark, came over and rapped on my window.

'Can't you read?'

'Yes. I can read.'

'Then get that car to hell out of here and don't come back.'

'No.'

He should have been warned then, but he wasn't.

'Right. You're for it,' and he took out his little black book and pencil. 'Name?'

I gave him my name.

'Occupation?'

'Advocate, and of this court the Sheriff.'

If it was not that I detest bullies I would have been sorry for the fellow. He apologised, he grovelled, he said that all he had been doing was to keep the space clear for me, but it was not enough.

I told him that it did not matter how he talked to me, but if he ever dared to talk like that to any member of the public I would get to hear about it and see that he was put out of the force. I wouldn't and couldn't, of course, but maybe it did some good.

The police, particularly in the west of Scotland are going through a rough time just now, and have been for some years. They have lost touch with the people they serve, and more importantly with their conception of themsleves as a peace keeping force. They are obsessed with the television shadow of the tough American cop. They act, rather than behave. When a policeman stops a speeding car, he is more likely to say to the driver, 'Where the hell do you think you're going?' than the polite,'Excuse me, sir'. The end result is not merely a speeding ticket. In the one case the citizen goes away with a grievance; in the other with an appreciation that the police have a tough job to do and are doing it in the service of us all. An ultimate analysis shows that it is the public who keep law and order, not the police, and a public who regard the police as an enemy are not going to help in the suppression of crime, particularly petty crime.

Every motorist is a potential juror. In criminal trials jurors decide who is telling the truth. It is a fact of human nature that the adrenalised human wants to talk. Any person charged with a crime is adrenalised and he is likely to make admissions of guilt. By the time he meets his solicitor he is appalled that he has made these admissions, and he denies them. In court it is his word against that of the police. There was a time when the police were almost always believed. That time is long past. Too many members of a jury have had rough words from the police and have had experience of them denying that they were rude. They no longer accept them as people of the utmost probity. I have often said to my wife that my ideal defence case is five truthful lay witnesses followed by five police witnesses, giving evidence of admissions that my client denies making. The public have become so doubtful of police evidence that there is a fifty fifty chance of an acquittal in such cases. While no experienced advocate depute will say so in public, many of them will not lead police evidence if they have sufficient evidence elsewhere. It is not right that the guilty should go unpunished because the police have so conducted themselves that juries are reluctant to believe them.

There is a greater danger to society than the guilty going free. That greater danger is of you, an innocent person being convicted. Do not think it couldn't happen to you. To the policeman, no one is above suspicion. Confessions play a great part in the conviction of the citizen. Almost invariably the confession is made to police officers. The citizen must be warned by the police that he is not bound to say anything but that anything he says will be taken down and may be used in evidence. It is not much of a safeguard. Thereafter the police often use both threats and promises to get a statement which fits the facts they already know about the crime. In Scots law there must be supporting evidence for any confession before a conviction can follow. But that supporting evidence can be found within the statement itself. If the statement holds facts

135

which could only have been known to the perpetrator of the crime, it is only common sense to allow proof of these facts to corroborate the admission he has made. Facts known to the police can be suggested by them in questioning, and when the final statement is written out, or even tape recorded, the bewildered suspect finds himself committed to saying that he saw something which was, in truth, known to the police, but not indeed to him. Out of his own mouth he has corroborated himself. It is called a special knowledge confession.

In a recent interview with the press, given after his retirement, Lord President Emslie assured the public that such a conviction as that of the Guildford Four could not happen in Scotland. I greatly respect Lord Emslie, but I must contradict him. A glance at the summing up of Mr Justice Donaldson in the trial of the Guildford Four shows how heavily the Crown relied on special knowledge confessions. It could happen in Scotland. Paradoxically it is most likely to happen in the most reprehensible of crimes. These are the crimes the police are under great pressure to solve. They form a view and look for evidence to support that view. God help you if you are the neighbour of a child who has been murdered. God help you if you have an Irish accent, and a bomb has gone off. Your safeguard is no longer the police. Your only safeguard is your counsel, and the good sense of Scottish juries. And the nature of such crime is so repugnant to decent people that juries are eager to convict. I fear for justice when I defend such crimes.

Let me give you a totally different scenario. You have a much-loved son who is foolish enough to be smoking cannabis. You worry but you are not going to make your son homeless, by throwing him out. You hope he will grow out of the habit. The police raid your house and they find two or three ounces of the substance. You are taken into the police station and the law says that you may be detained for six hours. You are only bound to give your name and address. You are entitled to have a solicitor informed. Little good does that do you, because he is not entitled to have access to you. On the way in to the police station in the police car, you are told that, 'You are really in the shit. You had better decide, and decide fast whether you are going to be a witness or a convict.' You are not used to being talked to like that. You are frightened. In the police station you give some basic information and a form is filled in. You do not know the name of a solicitor, and anyway the police tell you that no one will turn out at that time of the morning. You are told that you need not say anything, and you resolve not to. A friendly chap tells you that you are going to be locked up, but he will see what he can do for you. The cell door slams behind you. There is a concrete plinth on the floor, which may have a mattress on it, and there is a wooden bench. The place smells of vomit and urine. You can't believe that this is happening to you. Time passes. It is forever, because your watch has been taken away.

The door opens and a kind man takes you to a room. You remember that you need say nothing. 'Come on,' says the kind man. 'Your son has told us all about it. You had better clear yourself.' You still say nothing. 'Look,' says the kind man. 'I didn't want to do this but we've had to bring your wife in.' The door to the corridor is opened and you see your wife passing. She is in tears. 'Are you going to be a witness or are you going into the dock. Not just you, but your wife too.' You wonder what you should do. You know nothing except that your son has been smoking pot. The policeman says, 'And your younger children are being taken into care, all because you won't make a statement. Come on. Help us and then you can all go home.'

You see that the nice man has your shaving kit. 'That's mine,' you say. You have cracked. Quite unwittingly you have incriminated yourself. He draws a little package from it. 'Come on,' he says. 'I'll help you. Nobody can want to go back into that cell. You're a respectable man. Get it off your chest, and I personally will see that everything is all right with you and your wife.' He produces paper and pen.

'For some time my son has been smoking pot,' says the nice man. You go along with it. When you have finished you have given enough evidence against yourself to get you five years for possession with intent to supply drugs. And another detective constable is on the way for promotion.

Another variation has been used by Lords Advocate, who should know better. When a crime has been committed he charges also a wife or younger brother, and then lets it be known that the charge against the wife or brother will be dropped if the one believed to be the real culprit pleads guilty. I once had five cases like that in five months. I wrote in each case charging the Lord Advocate with abuse of his office. I got no reply until I sent one of the letters to the press. Since then I have not seen a case like that. I am not liked by Lords Advocate. Of course such charges are not prepared personally by the Lord Advocate. They are prepared by his servants. He is too busy with his political career to care.

The very name Lord Advocate is impressive. He sounds so great that people think he can't be challenged. In fact he is only a minor Minister of Government, so minor that no Lord Advocate of recent times has had a seat in the cabinet. I challenge the Lord Advocate again on another subject. Here and now I challenge him about an abuse that goes on day and daily. It is so common that I feel that I am wrong-headed in reporting it. Let the reader be the judge.

It is Crown office policy to charge almost every homicide as murder. Not all, but almost all. Thereafter negotiations take place between the Crown and the defence, and during the course of these the Crown may indicate that they are now willing to accept a plea of guilty to culpable homicide. This is a lesser but still grave crime. It does not attract the mandatory sentence of life imprisonment, which is the punishment for murder. It usually attracts imprisonment for many years. The choice is put to the accused through his counsel. The wretch must then elect whether he should plead guilty to the lesser charge, or go ahead and face trial on the murder charge. This is wrong. No person should be faced with such a choice. It is for the Crown to decide what charge he has to face. If the Crown are willing to accept a plea of guilty to the lesser crime, they should not seek a conviction for the graver one. No man should be forced into pleading guilty to a grave crime, by the fear that he might be convicted of a graver one. Remember, in all such crimes there is a defence. The defence is usually not that of a denial, although it might be. The defence is often that the act was done in self defence. The vital fact that the crime was regarded by the crown, for the purposes of negotiation, as one of culpable homicide cannot be brought before the jury. When they have the terrible job of deciding whether the matter is murder, culpable homicide, or no crime at all, that vital fact is not before them. The system is wrong, yet I seem to be alone in complaining of it.

These are the rotten apples, in the administration of justice, and in the trial of serious crime. Not all prosecutors are like that. Not all policeman are over zealous. Some are just plain brave. Come out Chief Inspector Adam Hay of Dumbarton, humble little man that you are. Leave the bowling club, and put on that dirty old raincoat of yours and your shy grin. I know you hate publicity and think you are just doing a job, but you are the bravest man I ever met in court. I am going to tell a story about you.

A drunken fool was playing Rambo. Naked to the waist, and with a bandolier of cartridges round his shoulder, a twelve bore in his hand, and a bottle or two of whisky in his belly, he shot his sister-in-law, almost severing her arm. He didn't know the gun was loaded. The occupants of the house assisted the injured woman away. The drunk, now mad with fear, telephoned to say that he would sell his life dearly, and the place was surrounded by armed police. Adam Hay was called in.

Unarmed, out of uniform, he walked up to the front door of

the house, opened it, and was confronted by the armed madman with the loaded shotgun in his hands.

'Cool it, son,' he said. And then he opened his jacket showing that he was unarmed. 'Gonna put the gun out of a window, and I'll come back and you and me'll walk to my car. No handcuffs. No rough stuff. Just you and me.'

Then he turned his back on the drink-crazed gunman and walked down the path, and stood with his hands in his dirty old raincoat pocket. Twenty minutes later the gun came out a window, and Adam Hay made his arrest, just as he had said he would.

I wrote to the Chief Constable about that. So far as I know Adam Hay never got any commendation, but I write his name with pride.

If they were all like Adam Hay a jury's job would be a much easier one, but they are not. There never yet has been a tyranny which has not found plenty of men and women willing to police it, and to do its bidding. The theory that the end justifies the means stains the thinking of far too many policemen. It is the job of advocates to expose that heresy to make the country a safer place for us all. The first line of defence against the police state is a strong criminal bar. This is more important today than it has ever been before. We have a centralised government thrusting policies down our throats which we don't want. One of the very first actions of that government, was to raise the pay of the police to a level far above that of the ordinary working man. I want to see the police well paid, but that action of the Government was a cynical and sinister one. In almost every other field of public service it cares not what wage is paid. A Government which pays its policemen more than its nurses may have got its priority right. If it has, it is a danger to us all.

12 The Free Fishers of Fairlie

LIFE CONTINUES, with both death and life. My father died in 1968, round about the time I was picking myself together again. He slipped away as though he had an appointment to keep elsewhere, as perhaps he had. He left me a little money, not much, thank God, but enough to put down for a house. I chose the little village of Fairlie on the Clyde coast. Still bewildered by events I decided to become a west of Scotland solicitor, and Fairlie was as good a place as any to choose, and better than most. I would need to pass an exam in accounting to become a solicitor, and serve a year's training. One day a sheriff, the next an apprentice. The position was ludicrous, and after six months, common sense prevailed, and I went back to the Bar.

Before returning to the Parliament House, accident, design, and the gods above provided an amusing interlude. Along the road from Fairlie is the village of Portencross. Daniel Defoe, best known for *Robinson Crusoe*, was an English spy, and travelled widely throughout Scotland just prior to the Union of 1707. His account of his travels make racy reading. He gathered together local stories wherever he went, and in his account of Ayrshire he tells how a Spanish Galleon foundered close in to the village of Portencross. I was skin-diving at that time, and to the amusement of the local press I attempted to raise finance to find the galleon. We never found it, but twenty years on the local tourist board has taken the matter seriously, and the search still goes on.

To keep myself while diving I took a job as a lorry driver at the power station then being built at Hunterston. While I was a lorry driver I formed an alliance with a belted Earl and his Countess, and no one could have been more kind to me. I became a constant visitor to Kelburn Castle, often making a quick change from my working clothes to do so. My meeting with them came about casually enough, though I will change the girl's name and nationality in case her husband reads this book.

I was eking out my modest lorry-driver's pay with some writing, and I had just sold an article for thirty-five pounds. That went quite a long way in the 1960s. Thus when some friends introduced me to a charming and beautiful American, I was able to say, 'Will you come to the Highlands Leezie Lindsay? Will you come to the Highlands with me?' She gave me a long slow look and I knew my weekend was made.

During our two days in the Highlands, which we both enjoyed immensely, the girl was very cagey as to where she was staying, and being a gentleman I did not enquire. On the conclusion of our liaison, she asked to be driven to Kelburn Castle, a type of address to which I was not accustomed. She was a house guest there. That Monday evening, when I had just returned from work my telephone rang. It was the Earl of Glasgow. He asked me if I would be good enough to step up to the castle. He wished to have a word with me.

My presbyterian conscience gave a flutter, but in such matters it is quite well trained. When I presented myself at the door of Kelburn, it was as much in curiosity as in fear. Sanham, the butler, showed me into the drawing-room and the Earl introduced himself, and introduced me to the Countess. Mary, my weekend friend was curled up on a sofa, reading a book and ignoring me, the traitress. In the event not a word was spoken about Mary's disappearance. Instead a great crystal goblet of whisky was put into my hand, enough to founder any lorry driver, and I thoroughly enjoyed my evening. For the rest of my time in Fairlie the telephone would often ring and I would be asked up to the castle for drinks and sometimes for dinner.

They were nearly old enough to be my parents and we became the best of friends. I do not think they knew just how badly I needed friends. I think they actually enjoyed my

142

company. Mary had been a paying guest, one of many who came to Kelburn from time to time. It was the only way they could keep the castle and the small estate together. Americans pay a small fortune for a week end with a real live Earl and Countess. The reason they had asked me up on the day I took Mary back to the Castle was they were curious to meet someone who was a greater attraction to an American than an Earl and Countess.

I look back with an enormous feeling of delight to that friendship. The family motto of the Boyles is carved above the fire place in the great drawing-room at Kelburn. It is *Dominus Providebit*, The Lord Will Provide, and when we got involved in any scheme and it was asked where the money would come from, I used to murmur unctiously, the Lord will provide, and the Earl would roar, 'Well this one won't'.

His name was being used to advertise Chivas Regal whisky in the States at the time, and it was not in short supply at Kelburn. They were just as good companions over a cup of coffee or a fish supper. Like all retired people they were lonely. You don't get to be a Rear Admiral, just because you are an Earl, although I suspect it helps, and I think they were missing the bustle of life. Certainly in David Niven's autobiography, he describes the Earl as one of the brightest young men ever to put on a midshipman's uniform. To retire to the peace of Ayrshire and entertain PGs, (paying guests) as they called their Americans, can't have been all that fun.

The three of us, the Earl, the Countess and the lorry driver fought a war as allies and had a famous victory. It is an example of how a little resolution and a little knowledge can prevail against the strongest enemy.

The Portencross peninsula, a lovely stretch of hill and agricultural land three miles from the windows of Kelburn Castle and jutting out into the estuary provided ideal land for a deep-water jetty on to which to discharge the new generation of cargoes from the new generation of ships. The international oil company Chevron Oil had its eye on it, and wanted to turn the peninsula into an oil terminal, build a deep-water jetty for supertankers, and put down oil storage tanks, from which the oil would be pumped away to their refineries elsewhere in Scotland. Attractive as that idea was in an area which even then had a high level of unemployment it had its drawbacks. One obvious one was that it would destroy the beauty of the Portencross Peninsula. It would incidentally destroy the view from the windows of Kelburn Castle, and from hundreds of smaller homes. More importantly, when it was completed it would provide employment for only a handful of men.

The worst of motives is always attributed to any objector to something new, particularly if he is an Earl. The Earl of Glasgow's family had always played its part in the local community. Largs golf course was held by the club on a peppercorn rent from the Glasgows, who had little more to live on than their bed and breakfast business and his naval pension. Many of the golfers were much richer than the Earl. A hundred years previously the family had nearly bankrupted itself during one of the Victorian trade depressions, by providing work for the unemployed. They had a needless wall built round the estate. Bits of it are still falling down and I expect it is a nightmare to maintain and impossibly expensive to remove. They built the Cathedral of the Isles in Millport for the same reason. I don't usually spur Rosinante to the aid of Earls, but Glasgow is an exception.

Now that Chevron Oil was coming, the Earl's view was that it would sterilise a prime site which could better be developed for something else. He was right. If Chevron Oil had not been defeated, we would not have got the ore terminal at Hunterston, and the Scottish steel industry would have been doomed. When the ore terminal was planned he did not oppose it, however much his view was spoiled.

There was a public inquiry going on at the time, to report to the Secretary of State for Scotland on all aspects of Chevron's

144

proposed development. Public Inquiries are all very well and I have taken part in many myself. The real decision is taken however, not at the inquiry, but behind the doors, and among the filing cabinets of some civil service department. We advocates are as nice a body of men as ever persuaded the Secretary of State to knock down an orphanage to make way for a supermarket. We are also the main beneficiaries of Public Inquiries. I advised Lord Glasgow to have nothing to do with the inquiry and to hit Chevron where it hurt most, and that was by fighting a long troublesome delaying action in the courts. I was not advising him as an advocate, only as a lorry driver.

If you want to injure someone get him off his own ground. Inquiries are the home ground of the multinationals. Wherever in the world they go, they are geared to deal with them. I dare say they have a department on the subject in their head office, and an ambitious young vice-president in charge. The Harvard Business School will have a lot to say about how to make the best of them. What they are not geared to do is to fight the common law of every country they may go to, and Scotland has a vigorous common law.

One night at Kelburn we were talking about the law. I had recently seen a report that a salmon had again been seen in the waters of the Clyde as far up as Renfrew, and of course the salmon in Loch Lomond have never died out. When salmon are coming up an estuary to spawn they keep close to the shores. The burns bring down a measure of fresh water, which forms a surface layer, and this first taste of fresh water excites the fish and stimulates it to press on to its breeding grounds in the gravels and reeds far upstream in the tributary burns. It stuck in my mind that salmon fishings are a separate estate in lands, that is they can be bought, sold and leased separately and I would have been surprised if an estate like Kelburn, with a frontage along the Clyde estuary did not have salmon fishing rights. I suggested to Lord Glasgow that he check up with his solicitor, and this proved to be the case. Now with a glass of Chivas Regal in my hand I let the idea flow.

'We've got them now. We form a small company. The company leases the salmon fishing rights, and we go to the courts and interdict Chevron Oil from interfering with the ancient rights of salmon fishing in the Clyde.'

The Earl and Countess looked very dubious.

'Where will we get the money for all this,' asked Lord Glasgow.

'The Lord will provide,' I murmured, and got the expected roar in reply.

'And what if we lose?' asked the Countess. 'Couldn't Chevron Oil bankrupt us if we had to pay the costs of their lawyers too. Lawyers can be very expensive.'

'The best defence to an action of payment, is to have no money. And our company will have no money. We will raise only enough to pay our own lawyers.'

Then I explained about the liabilities of a company, and the freedom from liability of the shareholders and directors if they took proper care. Mind you, being the directors of a simulate company is not without risk. Chevron Oil was big enough to be a worthwhile enemy, and the preservation of the Portencross Peninsula was worth fighting for. There is no fight without risk.

I suggested that they did not take my word for it. It would not take much to form a company and the company could then take the opinion of Queen's Counsel.

'And what do we call the company?' one of them asked.

'The Gentlemen Adventurers of Portencross,' I suggested. That was the whisky taking effect.

The Earl gave one of his characteristic roars. 'I'll be the laughing stock of the House of Lords as it is with this mad idea,' he said, 'without provoking it with a name like that.'

'What about the Free Fishers of Fairlie?' There was a long thoughtful silence. 'It sums it all up. A small free people

146

against a great multi-national corporation,' and the Free Fishers of Fairlie we became.

The company was formed with myself and the Countess as the directors. A few of their friends put in fifty pounds each and senior counsel's opinion was sought. It coincided with mine. We sought and got our interim interdict in the Court of Session. Predictably Chevron Oil were put into disarray. This was not fighting fair. They flew over a team of lawyers to London to find out what it was all about. The team searched round London, and could find no trace of the case. Someone then remembered that Scotland had its own system of law, and they came to Edinburgh. They saw that they had a long case on their hands, far longer than a public enquiry would take and they decided to withdraw and go elsewhere. I believe that it was the Free Fishers of Fairlie which drove them away. It was not the last straw which broke the camel's back. It was a lance held in the hands of free people, and it did not break.

The Free Fishers of Fairlie was reminiscent of the fight John MacCormick and I had together over the Queen's title, and the fight I had alone to be sworn in as an advocate without the numeral. I was pursuing the same ends with the Free Fishers, only this time it was with an Earl and Countess beside me. You meet a nice class of person when you're a lorry driver.

13 Kirriemuir:
Scotland's Finest University

HAVING EXHAUSTED all the facilities of Fairlie, in 1970 I came back once again to Edinburgh. It had not changed from my last appearance there two years before. People said 'Hello, Ian,' as though yesterday and today had been telescoped together, and no time had passed. In the long history of the law that is all it was. For me, however, Edinburgh brought back all the old memories of happier days, and still I grieved. Edinburgh, and the Parliament House was only a base from which to move on to something else. I was shortly to get a job in Kirriemuir as a museum curator, but I did not know that then. I stuck it out in Edinburgh for two unhappy years. Like the family dog I was always on the wrong side of the door. Yet life began to come together again with closer friends.

Among these friends was Ada Kay. One night I went down to the Gateway Theatre to see a new play. It was, of all unlikely things on a text from Thucydides, 'and from Thermopylae one man returned and he was ostracised'. Now and again in the live theatre life is suspended and we breathe a magic air. We are no longer us, we are the gods watching the mortals. We watch, pitying, hoping, and suddenly proud that one or two have cast off their mortality and are fit to walk and talk in our company. From the moment the curtain went up on *The Man From Thermopylae* it showed itself to be that sort of play. As each curtain fell, a long sigh went through the house as the audience disengaged itself, and there was a pause before the applause broke out.

It has one particular line which is far beyond any applause. It is a line that has meant a great deal to me. It is in my in-built thesaurus and every now and again, in some form or another I am surprised to hear myself spell it out to a jury. Yet it is the basis of all law.

'Deny justice to the meanest in the community, and which person amongst us is safe?'

That is not an accurate quotation, yet it is how I remember it. For twenty years that line has been my close companion and my ever present reminder of what my job is about. I sought and found Ada Kay. You might have expected Ada to be some desiccated Edinburgh spinster, high on Greek, who had hit off a play instead of a recipe book, and it had been a chance in a million success. Nothing of the kind. When she opened her door to me there stood a beautiful young woman, and no recipe writer. Ada had learned her craft with the BBC.

In the lonely years Ada Kay was one of my constant companions. People who live ordinary lives should never decry the convictions of others. Ada believes with the utmost conviction that she is the reincarnation of James IV, our king who fell at Flodden. The fact that she is a tall redhead with a body like Diana's, not Diana the Princess but Diana the goddess, cannot shake her Royal Grace's conviction. I never attempted to, so I became a courtier of a king, and of a King of Scotland at that. This new Jamie the IV, like the late medieval king himself, was aye into new ideas, and new things, and her/his company was like embroidering a tapestry with bright threads of thought. In her autobiography, Ada recalls how I took her to the fo'c'sle of a Newhaven fishing boat, and there abandonned her. I don't recall that, but I was often aboard Newhaven fishing boats, and if she says so, it will be true. One of my most abiding memories is of taking her to L'Aperitif, then one of Edinburgh's most fashionable restuarants, and a great haunt of the Bar. She turned up dressed as a rennaissance king, with a golden circlet round her head, and in a long, flowing, royal, purple gown. She was magnificent, but she was not Edinburgh. At that royal court of Ada/Jamie there were, of course, ladies-in-waiting. I married one of them.

Marriage is a strange institution and I say little of my second marriage. The lady has reverted to her former name, and that is the best comment that could in the circumstances be made on me. Many worse might be more truthful. By the time I set off for Kirriemuir she was quite ready not to come with me. She divorced me some time later.

Kirriemuir was one of my wiser choices. I went there in 1972. It is the birthplace of J.M. Barrie. The birthplace is run by the National Trust for Scotland, and the office of curator became vacant. I applied for it and was appointed. The National Trust for Scotland seems to me to be an awfully English sort of institution. The voices that come over the telephone from their headquarters in Edinburgh's Charlotte Square terrify me, with their ya-ya and yo-yo, but the institution is sound enough at heart. I hope they persist in a policy of employing weary men, and would-be authors in their smaller properties. The job is not taxing; the pay is not great; but the peace of these small Scottish towns is elsewhere unknown.

I was very happy at Kirriemuir, and peace came dropping low. The property is a weaver's cottage and at that time only two of the four rooms were open to the public. It had been combined with the cottage next door, and there was a neat little house for the curator. I moved in, and on the first night there, sitting with my bits of unpacked gear around me, all on my own, I started to bone up on Barrie. In my hand was Barrie's most famous work, next to *Peter Pan*. It was his Rectorial address on *Courage*. A knock on the door interrupted me. Opening hours for the museum, were long past, and it was indeed quite late. No one in Kirrie knew me. I wondered who it could be. I put down *Courage*, opened the door, and looked into the night.

Courage, and the right of ordinary people to their place in the sun are worth serving. That night's visitor gave me the opportunity to serve both. My visitor was a twelve-year old

150

local boy, asking to be shown round. Nothing like that ever happened again. The locals are not interested in Barrie, and I do not know, and never found out what brought him to my door late that night. Perhaps he came, impelled by the gods themselves. I showed him round the birthplace, telling him what little I then knew of it. At the end he thanked me politely, said ,'My Daddy's got the VC' and vanished into the dark.

I was intrigued by my visitor and the next day I asked round to find out about the boy, and particularly about the VC.

'That must have been Dick Burton's boy,' someone said, and I asked who Dick Burton was.

Dick Burton lived on the other side of the town and was a labourer in the builder's yard at the back of the birthplace, only a few yards away. He was a tall quiet Englishman, slow moving, seemingly slow thinking, the type that seems in awe at everything that is happening around him. Perhaps he was just still glad to be alive. At close of day we went for a pint together. When I told him of his son's visit he smiled. He gave the impression that he was proud of his son, and who would not be?

At last I brought the conversation round to the subject of the VC.

' Oh yes,' he said. 'Ive got the VC' and he pulled out the little wallet with the card which is provided to all VCs to prove beyond doubt that they have received the highest award for gallantry that any country can offer.

We were getting on famously, and I was bold enough to ask him what he had got it for. Remember, this was twenty-five years after the war had ended.

'I don't know,' he said. 'It was in the Eighth Army in Italy. One day they just said," Burton. You're out," and pulled me out of the line. I thought I was being crimed for something, but I had nothing much on my conscience. Then they flew me home and the King gave me the VC. I wasn't objecting.'

'But what for?' I persisted, and he just shrugged.

'They just gave it to me,' he said.

What about your citation in the *London Gazette*?' I asked. 'That would tell you what you got it for.'

' What's the *London Gazette*?

If I had not myself been a ranker I might have left it at that, and concluded that here was the stiff upper-lip English pose that great events must be minimised, and that a gentleman does not talk about them in pubs. But I had met Dick Burton, and a most patently nice, humble, honest man he was. It seemed to me that he truly did not know what he had received the supreme award for, and what's more, had never expected to be told. The suspicion grew in me that the presentation of Dick's VC had gone off with typical military precision, except that no one had bothered to tell Dick what it was all about. It is only officers who use the phrase, 'typical military precision'. We rankers have only one word for that glib phrase. It is the word 'snafu'. An acronym for, 'situation normal all fucked up'. Something had to be done about Dick and his award of the Victoria Cross. Edinburgh Castle was the place to do it.

The military museum at Edinburgh Castle keeps the records of the Scottish Regiments, and a great deal more besides. I borrowed the fare from my mother who had come to live with me, and went down to Edinburgh to ask them about the gazetting of a Victoria Cross to a Private soldier in the Sherwood Forresters sometime in 1944. Within a few minutes they dug it out for me, and gave me a photostat to take back to Kirrie, where I had it framed. When I tried to pay for the framing the lady in the shop shook her head and walked away. I thought she was weeping. Maybe she was weeping with pride for that simple man.

That night I met Dick in a pub and handed it to him.

He read it.

It described how his company was pinned down by fire from two machine gun posts, and was suffering heavy casualties. How Private Richard Burton, firing a Bren gun from the hip ran forward and silenced one, and then regardless of his own safety, turned on the other and, his Bren gun now being empty, silenced it first with grenades, and then in fierce hand-to-hand fighting. There was much more. It took up the whole front page of the *London Gazette*.

Dick read it slowly. 'I remember that,' he said with wonder. 'But I didn't think anyone else did.'

Not knowing what to say, I made a banal pub remark. 'You must have been on the vino that day.'

'No,' said Dick, without meaning to rebuke me. 'I was just angry at seeing my mates killed.'

He had long since sold his medal, but maybe the framed *London Gazette* still hangs on his wall. It did not mean much to Dick but he took it home to show to his wife and boy. It would mean a lot to them. That's the sort of thing you can do as a museum curator.

The job of museum curator was among the most fascinating things I have ever done. Upstairs, in the little room where J.M. Barrie had been born there was a collection of manuscripts and costumes. A great many of the latter related to Peter Pan. After half a season dealing with Peter Pan, and the school kids who were brought in droves to 'do a project' I wished I had the power of King Herod. Girls as well as boys, I could have slain them all. There was really nothing there to interest kids. In that respect I could only do a poor best. But I dug up a bit more about Robert Falcon Scott.

One of the lesser known facts about Barrie is that Robert Falcon Scott, when dying in the Antarctic wrote his last letter to him. It was found beside Scott's body in that tent in the Antarctic, a long way from Kirriemuir. The full text had only recently been made public, but the actual letter, written with a pencil held laboriously in a frost-bitten hand, in the tent in the blizzard, had been seen by only a very few. It seemed to me that the actual sight of the handwriting, as well as the content

153

of the letter might be something that people would want to see. I certainly did. Barrie was Peter Scott's, godfather, so I wrote to him, asking if the birthplace of his godfather might have a photostat of his father's letter, and he sent me one. If I had been there a little longer I might have got the precious letter itself. I had a little case made for the photostat and put it on the window sill of the upper room.

'My Dear Barrie,' it begins, 'we are pegging out in a pretty comfortless spot. Hoping this letter may be found and sent on to you.' As the handwriting becomes ever more shakey and wavers to an illegible conclusion he tells of his great respect and friendship for Barrie. I defy anyone to read that document without being deeply moved, both by the words of the letter and by the resolution of the writer alone in his tent with two dead companions to get his message across to his friend before the pencil fell from his fingers. To bring such matters before the public is one of the things a museum is about.

I set an eight minute tape playing in the upstairs room of the museum. That is about all a visitor will take. It left me free to speak to people downstairs. Kirriemuir is on the road to nowhere, so all the visitors had made a detour to come. They had some interest in the subject and were not merely there to get out of the rain. Every now and again a scholar would turn up, pretty often an American, and that was a rare treat for me. I learned much from them and, since I knew my subject and was able to talk with some knowledge of other playwrights and compare them to Barrie, perhaps I gave something also. Certainly, so far as the National Trust was concerned, my charge went to the top of the league of people who joined the Trust at the various properties.

Poor Barrie. He buried his talents in a napkin in an English park. He was so determined to be an English gentleman that his ability got mugged somewhere in Kensington Gardens. Never condemn him for his kailyard portrait of Scotland. Scotland endures. When he wrote the Kailyard stuff it was for money and we know what he wanted to do with his money. He wanted to give his mother an egg every morning for her breakfast. They were that poor. He achieved that ambition, but the memory of his family's early poverty never left him. Writing for money became a fixation. Only once the mask drops and he lets himself go. In *Peter Pan* he was writing for fun, and the real Celtic fantasy comes through. The tragedy of the man is that for all the fertility of his mind he had no one but the stuffed shirts in the late Victorian and Edwardian stalls to write for. There was no great audience calling for great plays, and he had not the vision and endurance of a MacDiarmid to create one.

I have my own vision of the pain of the lonely little man trudging back from the King's Theatre to the Caledonian Hotel in Edinburgh, after the first night of *The Boy David*, his last forgotten play, knowing that he had failed, not only with that play, but in life also. In *The Boy David*, a manuscript of which is in the birthplace, we see a series of embarrassing stage tricks. It is as though Barrie were saying, 'You can fool an audience all the time. Here's how to do it.' A lawyer talking about Barrie, has to make a constant plea in mitigation.

Donald Ross, then the Dean of the Faculty of Advocates, was generous enough to keep in touch with one of his wayward flock. He came to visit the birthplace with his wife. He is now the Lord Justice Clerk and I remember saying to them what sums up the job of curator at Barrie's birthplace. One makes a constant plea in mitigation of the sentence passed on him by the judgment of history. Plead as you will, apart from *Peter Pan* and his address on *Courage* he lost his way. His genius became a mere talent, the greatest might-have-been in Scottish literary history. The local feeling about him was interesting. They felt he had let the town down. He had gone off and become an English gent. That is a harsh view, but not without justice. It is the judgment of his own folk in Kirriemuir

I loved Kirriemuir. While on its outskirts there was the

usual froth of executives, the main town still centred round the linen mill. It had supplanted the hand loom weaving which had been the town's staple. There was always some flax growing in the flower bed before the cottage, so the kids could see where their civilisation came from. I had little need to do more than that. The town gardener was a man of pride, and he kept my flowerbeds in bloom from May to October. They may not have liked Barrie, but they took any stranger who loved Kirrie to their hearts, and I loved Kirrie.

For such a tiny town, it had two weekly newspapers, each in grim competition. Willie Ogilvie founded, owned, wrote, reported for, edited, printed and distributed the *Kirriemuir Herald*. In his spare time he took in the advertisements and ran a printing business. I went to see him on my first day there. I had primed myself with an intelligent question and asked him why his paper carried no death notices.

Willie pushed his bunnet to the back of his head, scratched it, and gave his reply. 'Nae deaths in Kirrie last week.'

In no time at all I was writing a column for the paper, and getting printers' ink on my hands again. It was an old shop, like the MacKenzie's in Anderston, or like my own in Castle Wynd. I was at home.

It was a rich community, far far beyond anything money can ever buy. I even made friends with the local minister and had long discussions with him on Kierkegaard. I remember the minister's phrase, 'Life without faith is a knotless thread'. He did not convert me, and I am glad to say I did not convert him. I admired him very much, and I except him from all my diatribes against the cloth, many of which I confess are ill-deserved.

On the nearest Sunday to Midsummer's Day, the day on which the Battle of Bannockburn was fought, he preached a sermon at my request on the first and second verses of the triumphant fortieth chapter of Isaiah.

'Comfort ye, comfort ye my people', saith your God.
'Speak ye comfortably to Jerusalem and cry unto her
that her warfare is accomplished, that her iniquity
is pardoned: for she has received of the Lord's
hand double for all her sins'.

It is the collect for the Day of the Feast of Saint John,
Midsummer's Day. It was read in some form by the padres just
before the Scots spearsmen made their advance down the hill,
in schiltrom form, to receive cavalry. When Edward saw the
ranks of the spearsmen break, and the spears waver and dip in
their lines, he thought the Scots were kneeling in surrender.
They weren't. They were kneeling to take their blessing.

We had Charles Pilkington Jackson, the sculptor of the
Bruce Statue at the Heritage Centre at Bannockburn to read the
lesson. I got Dick Burton there with great difficulty, nearly in
handcuffs, always about to bolt. I forget what I was trying to
demonstrate. Perhaps that if England can remember its
victories, so can we. But the spectacle of Dick and me sitting
stiffly, side by side, each as uncomfortable as the other, must
have caused great merriment. You could have written a reel
about us.

Kirriemuir is the centre of the Angus Strathspey and Reel
Society, whose fiddle music is world famous. Rightly, its
members have a fine conceit of themselves. When Yehudi
Menuhin came to play with them he expressed, like the great
gentleman he is, his diffidence in playing with such a
distinguished company of musicians.

The reply must have disconcerted even Sir Yehudi. The first
violin told him, 'Just you sit doon there atween Jock and me.
Follow us and ye'll dae fine. We've pit ye atween the twa best
fiddlers in Angus.'

The Angus Strathspey and Reel Society helped me to raise
money for the birthplace. The birthplace is an unendowed
property, which means that, other than the general funds of

the National Trust, there is no money to keep it up. It is therefore a considerable burden on the Trust to maintain it. While it would have taken me a long time to make it self supporting I tried to make a start towards that end. The Strathspey and Reel Society generously indicated that they were willing to help and I tried to identify three other factors which would combine Barrie with local interests and bring an audience along.

The first was cricket. Kirrie thinks it invented cricket. Whatever the truth may be, a fierce Saturday afternoon cricket is played on the hill above the cemetry. The Kirrie Club was always at or near the top of the local league. Barrie had been a cricketer, and had his own London team, The Allahakbarries, a collection of literary figures, judiciously strengthened by the odd professional.

The second factor was some part of Barrie's own work. To mount a play was far beyond the financial resources available, which were quite simply none. However there was his address as Lord Rector of St Andrews University, the one on *Courage*, which has already been mentioned. No modern paying audience would sit through it without throwing stones, but I thought something might be done with it if we had the right performer.

The third factor was the right performer. She was Sarah Churchill. She had once previously been in Kirriemuir, and through a combination of circumstances too dull to recite here, had caused a riot and been asked to take the first train home. I have a fellow feeling for anyone who has had that experience. I thought she might come back. An advertisement in the personal column of the London *Times*, asking her to get in touch brought an almost immediate reply, and she accepted an invitation to appear at a charity concert. I then issued a challenge to the Kirriemuir Cricket Club to meet the Allahakbarries in mortal combat. The local hall was booked for the Angus Strathspey and Reel Society on the evening of the

158

cricket match, and I sweated blood over a fifteen minute precis of Barrie on *Courage*, for Sarah Churchill to read.

The great day went well. The Allahakbarries drove to the field in a procession of vintage cars, myself in the back of an open Rolls Royce, lifting my cricketer's cap to the crowds. Ever a fraud, it was a Scottish internationalist's cap, which I had no right to wear, but neither had I any right to captain the Allahakbarries as I am no cricketer. I forget who won. I think we did. We played twelve aside, and four of my side had played for Scotland. I bowled one over. Kirrie did not make many runs off me. The ball never got near enough for the batsman to hit it. The square leg umpire caught one of my full tosses, and threw it into the air, to my great mortification, and the cheers of the crowd.

That evening the Strathspey and Reel Society did us proud. So did Sarah Churchill. We made quite a bit of money for the birthplace, but already my time there was drawing to a close. I had only another year to serve, but when I left it was in happier circumstances than I left Zambia.

Two years at Kirriemuir was like taking a degree in humanity at a great university. I recommend it to everyone.

14 Life is Worth a Venture

THERE WAS ONE MORE EXPLOIT in me before I left Kirriemuir. In 1960, twelve years before my time at Kirrie, I had spent a few days canoeing on Loch Lomond with Bob Grieve, or Professor Sir Robert Grieve as he is better known. Memories of these days came back to me as I thought how to raise more money for the birthplace. In his younger days Bob was a notable outdoors man, and rock-climber. When someone leads on the rope on a face not hitherto climbed he narrates the route for the *Scottish Mountaineering Club Journal* and is given the privilege of naming it. Bob pioneered many routes including one on the day that his first grandchild was born. As a result somewhere on a Scottish hill there is a climb called 'Grandfather's Gully'. I am no climber, but I enjoy canoeing. It was Bob who taught me.

Bob was later to become the first Chairman of the Highlands and Islands Development Board. At that time he was a senior civil servant so we had much to disagree about and we did. Civil servants and my anarchy are sometimes incompatible. It was all good humoured banter but sadly our views differed so much in later years that acrimony set in. He is the only friend I have ever fallen out with over a difference of opinion. May we both yet live long enough to make it up.

One of the many things we discussed without falling out was canoe journeys. Bob reckoned that it would be possible to canoe from the Atlantic to the North Sea. We decided that coming up the Clyde would not do. Not to cheat, we had to start from the Atlantic seaboard. There was the obvious route along the Great Glen, but that meant using the Caledonian Canal, and we decided that that too was cheating. Oban had to be the starting point. For years the ambition to canoe across Scotland lay not quite dormant in my mind. Now that I was trying to raise money for Barrie's birthplace the idea came back to me.

After my first season there the birthplace needed lime-washed. Its white harled walls were dingy. The estimates for the job were frightening, and without some sort of scaffolding it was impossible to do it myself. Besides that sort of work done by an amateur takes a long time. Because of the weather it can only be done in the tourist season. Better to get it done by experts. Quick in. Quick out. There are still people like that in Kirriemuir. Headquarters could not afford it so there was nothing for it but to set to and raise the money myself. I decided on an early spring crossing of Scotland by canoe, sponsored by my friends in Kirrie to raise the money. Oban to Kirriemuir was the challenge. The door closed on the last visitor at the end of October, and there was nothing to be done but start preparing for it.

The first thing was to get myself fit. I had had no exercise all summer and was soft as a ball of wool. My mother, told me to take it easy. What mother doesn't? The first day I walked ten miles and came back tired. The second ten again and came back more tired. The next twenty-five and, when I was off the hill and back on the road, only five miles from home, a car stopped and offered me a lift thinking I was ill. I kept on and came home staggering. After that things got better. A fencing stob, looted from somewhere, and carried on the twenty or more miles I did every day strengthened my wrists. I've tried to toughen myself up as quickly as that since then. It hasn't worked; it's nearly killed me. The great outdoors has to be treated with respect.

An outdoor centre in Dundee loaned a canoe. It was my first experience of the welfare state. Not wanting to drown I also borrowed the top half of a wet suit. It had its own buoyancy so I did not need a life jacket. A little ballet skirt which goes round your waist and stretches round the cockpit coaming keeps the spray and rain out. As there were some road portages to be made, a set of wheels was required. Ed Irvine a master in the local school made them for me. He is one of

Kirrie's great generous thrawn characters. They stowed between my knees. He also made me, riches beyond dreams to any canoeist, a tailor-made paddle. A small tent, a sleeping bag and some modest provisions made me entirely self-sufficient. All the above cost me nothing. It is a good thing because I had nothing to give. A museum curator is a king, but like royalty he carries no money. Practice was now necessary.

I practised on Forfar loch a few miles from Kirrie, pushing the canoe there and back on Ed's cradle. Later I got more ambitious and went down the Isla on it. There was always a change of clothing in the canoe in case of a capsize. A sealed polythene bag kept it dry. Often the canoe and the spare clothes were left in bushes by the riverside. One day the bag was opened and the clothes scattered. Enquiry revealed that it had been done by the local gamkeeper on the instructions of the landowner. He wanted to discourage me from using 'his' water. He wasn't a Scotsman so I didn't bother to seek him out to have it out with him. It sometimes takes quite a time for incomers to learn the habits of civilisation. I now had to attract sponsors, but this was easy. The Kirriemuir Round Table, and the Venture Scouts took over.

Early that spring the Venture Scouts had a recruiting drive in the Square at Kirrie and my canoe featured in it. There was a map of the route up on a board, so that sponsors could see where we would go. Mr Lowson, who ran a local painting business had painted her blue, and put the crest of the National Trust on bow and stern. She was called *Mary Rose* from the character in Barrie's play who kept returning. I was very proud of her. The birthplace reopened at the end of March, so the choice of when to go was made for me. In Scotland March can sometimes be a fine month. Spring comes late but the land lingers like a late sleeper in a winter which is cold but often benign. March 1973 was one of these months. Just before I left a telegram arrived at the birthplace. It was from my three children. It said, 'Good luck. Life is worth a venture.'

Life is Worth a Venture

The venture started at five o'clock one morning. Kirriemuir Round Table had arranged overnight transport for *Mary Rose* and me to Oban. It was in a freezer van, but I sat snuggly with the driver, sleeping most of the way, as I had to catch the morning tide. When I wakened we were within sight of Connel Bridge. I did not know it then but I was to live the happiest years of my life within sight of that bridge. I was nearly home again.

My route lay out from Oban, past the cliffs of Ganavan and round into Loch Etive. It is a steep-to rocky coast and no place for a lone slalom canoe in March. A canoe is invisible from any distance and no one knew I was going. It is a tidal coast and they were spring tides, that is tides at their highest and fastest. As planned I caught the tide out of Oban and it took me round into Loch Etive. A capsize on that leg would have killed me.

Beneath Connel Bridge, at the mouth of Loch Etive, there is a tidal race said to be the fastest in the British Isles. It is like a waterfall and is called the Falls of Lora. A shelf of rock runs three-quarters of the way across the Loch and the tide rushes in and out like a train. There was a flood tide with me but I wisely put into the landing stage at the Dunstaffnage Arms to wait for slack water. While standing by my canoe a television reporter approached with a camera on his shoulder. He wanted to see me shoot the Falls. It is one thing to canoe through white water for fun and quite another thing to do so in a canoe over-ladened for a cross-country trip. I nearly refused but he said he had a deadline to meet, and there were my sponsors to think about, so I went. We shot under the bridge like a torpedo, white water round my ballet skirt. I tried to miss the whirlpool on the south shore, hit the edge of it and capsized. The man got his pictures all right, but it was distinctly hairy for the canoeist.

There's a story to tell about that capsize. I wish I could make a fine song and sing it, because I fell in the water and I fell in love. I am no song-maker, but it is a fine story. The story is about how I swam ashore and met Jeannette, and how she became my wife. It is a happy story which I am saving to tell at the end of this chapter, although everything else I did on that trip after meeting Jeannette was just an anticlimax, just a plod-on. There was a journey to finish, and it was a long lonely road.

The journey took me up Loch Etive to Kinlochetive and after that there was the long portage to Loch Baa. Somewhere on Loch Etiveside I made camp. It is remote country which I was often to fly over, but I never spotted the exact place. It was too remote for English landlords, so I wasn't bothered by them. At the top of the Loch I rigged up Ed's wheels, put the canoe on it and started out. It is eighteen miles from the head of Loch Etive to Loch Baa on the Moor of Rannoch, and they went by in a dream. I was fit and the miles strode by me. *Mary Rose* sat like a baby in her cradle, and I sang songs to her.

I could have sung songs to the country I was passing through, and I probably did. It must be one of the most beautiful parts of the world. In Glen Etive Deirdre of the Sorrows had her orchard, and the river Etive still sings of her. The Great Shepherd at the head of the Glen, and Ben Starav at the foot saw her, as they saw the Sons of Uisneach and the first tentative coming of the Gaels, and later their intermarriage with the Norsemen. See Glen Etive and you have seen a great part of Scotland in miniature.

See Glen Etive, but the seeing pauses a moment like a shadow across the face of a hill, for it has all been loved as we love it, since our first forefathers came slowly north, ten thousand years ago, following the retreating ice of the last ice age. They loved the land as we love it. They were never exterminated. Their blood mixed with the blood of incomers, as our blood mixes with the blood of incomers today, and never a would-be conquerer but left someone behind, conquered by the beauty of it all. They saw and loved the same things that the Gaels sang about and still sing about, two thousand years after their first coming. They wondered at the long long other-landscapes of Caithness, and they felt the sudden lift of the heart you and I feel, when you come up the Irvine Water by Louden Hill, and on to the Avon and get your first glimpse of Tinto and the Border Hills. We succeed and are succeeded but the love of Scotland is older than the *Book of Genesis*. We do not just travel when we go about Scotland, we walk through time.

On the moor of Rannoch the very heart of time lurches. It is immense, endless, silent. There is no road. May there never be one. We Scots don't take much to looking at our shrines through glass, and certainly not through the glass of a car windscreen. That March of 1973 was the first time I crossed the moor. The day was blue, clear, and seemed iron hard, but the million burns which criss-cross it were unfrozen. All the growth had been beaten flat by the winter's rain. There were no midges and no tourists. Tourists can't cross unless they walk, although in a sort of savage serenity of tolerance the moor permits passage to north and south. On the east the railway floats on beds and branches, bound in faggots to hold the permanent way on the shuddering peat. On the west the road marches alongside the mountains.

Mary Rose and I trundled through those mountains, hills they are always called in Scotland, and reached Loch Baa. There I dismantled the bogey and put it back into the canoe. The peaty waters of the loch shone a cold rippled blue. Dipping the paddles rhythmically I set off across into the wilderness. You can't look back in a canoe. If you do you capsize, but you can turn it round. From where I had come the snow-covered peaks were like a barrier. It was a marvel to have come through them. There was no sound except the dip, dip of my paddles in the peat brown water of the loch.

Loch Baa was soon crossed and then came the portage down the Avon Baa. On the map it looked canoeable, but it proved to be a series of deep pools with short rocky falls between. I had to portage the whole way, sometimes over the shoulder of a hill, using my compass and laying out a string of posessions to keep me in line. It is only two miles but it took me ten hours. I greeted the outflow of the Avon Baa into Loch Laidon with relief. I made Rannoch Station just as night was falling.

From Rannoch Station down into Loch Rannoch and down the River Tummel, ever portaging round the Hydro Board dams, brought me into more populous country. One of the great joys of a trip like this is the people you meet. The newspapers had written that I was on my journey, and there had been the capsize at the Falls of Lora on television. I seemed to be doing something that many people had wanted to do, but I don't think anyone had. When people saw me from the banks and bridges they stopped what they were doing to wave and sometimes shout,'Good luck, Ian'. Even just a wave of the hand is an acknowledgment of our common humanity. In many ways it was a tour through my own people. Going round Pitlochry dam people came from nowhere to help me with the awkward portage.

From Pitlochry the way went on down the Tummel past where my parents used to live at Ballinluig, and through the pool where long ago I swam with a Dutch girl, my first love. Then it was into the Tay, down to Kinclaven Bridge, and the turn up the Isla. I could have gone on down the Tay and out to the North Sea, but this voyage had to end at Kirriemuir. From the Isla a tributary called the Water of Dean runs north-east to Glamis, and Glamis is only four miles from Kirriemuir. The Water of Dean is scarcely canoeable, but by means of dragging *Mary Rose* over the shallower parts and pulling her behind me where she would just float I reached the bridge just below Glamis Castle. I had waded the last few miles. It was a heave to get her up on to the road and to get the bogie underneath her. She was a tattered lady by this time, badly scarred and patched with broad strips of sticking plaster. The bogie wheels were rickety, and their spokes were also bound with sticking plaster. They only just made it to Kirriemuir.

It was before regionalisation and Kirriemuir was still a Burgh of Barony. The provost met me at the Burgh Boundary. The boot of his car was like a licensed premise, as Para Handy would have said, and we toasted the town, the Birthplace and above all *Mary Rose.* She was a gallant little craft and I had grown to love her. It was not a journey to the North Pole, but it had given a lot of simple people a lot of simple pleasure. They felt they were part of it and in many ways they were.

Kind as the Provost was, I was anxious to get away from him. I had a telephone call to make. I had to telephone to Connel. To Jeannette, the woman I met when I swam ashore out of the Falls of Lora, coming ashore as a stranger from the sea. We Scots love as we fight. We give no quarter, least of all to ourselves. After love of me died in Sheila, my first real love, it flamed on burning in me for nine whole years. The embers still burnt me until I met Jeannette. A great affection for Sheila is still there. I have been lucky. To have been consumed once at the stake may come to many men, but twice to meet the same fire and fury is given only to those whom the Gods love, and you know what usually happens to them. They die young, and are moderately lamented.

There is little moderation in the Scots character, and none at all in the Scotsman in love. Not wisely, but too well, is the way an Englishman might describe our behaviour. He may be right for him, but not a syllable is there in it for us Scots. To hell with moderation and doing things wisely and well. Down with, until death do us part and in sickness and in health, and all the lovely words of Cranmer and Latimer. Words. These are only words. I have loved and fought twice and the hunger of the blood has sung in my ears and the wind of the shouting has rung in my ears, all reason lost. Far beyond word or reason, blinded and in red blood we stand. We draw cold steel and never look behind us. That is what being in love is like. That is why I had to hurry and telephone Connel.

The village of Connel gets its name from a Gaelic word

meaning 'whirlpool'. Just below the church on the south bank the flood tide comes close to the shore and a massive pool is formed perhaps fifty yards across. There the flood tide races round and round. In a canoe you are nearly at surface level. Looking down into that pool is like looking down into a great circulating black mine. It isn't like that, but that's what it seems like.

When I came shooting under the bridge towards that pool, I paddled desperately for the north shore. Perhaps I paddled too desperately and missed a beat. That alone can cause a capsize. Perhaps the edge of the pool caught the bow and threw it round. For a moment I looked at the water as it curled like a glistening black line above my eyes, and then I was in.

There is only one way to get out of a whirlpool with a canoe, and that is to put one hand into the cockpit and swim the bow to the edge so that it catches in the still water, and then the circulating water should throw you out. It did. With luck it threw me out on the south side, and from there I was able to swim with *Mary Rose* to the rocky beach. I pulled her up to high water mark, not an easy job when she was full of water, and I had not the strength left to turn her end for end and shake the water out. I sat down to rest. Then I got my tent out, put it up and got into my sleeping bag, too tired even to take off my rubber jacket and wet clothes. There was no one about. The cameraman, seeing me swim ashore, had gone off with his pictures.

I was still shivering with cold and perhaps had a touch of hypothermia. The best, and traditional cure for hypothermia is two naked girls in bed with you, but I have never found two to give me the treatment. And Connel girls would take some persuading. The sleeping-bag did not seem to be doing me much good so I got out, leaving it damp from my wet body, and went up to the Falls of Lora Hotel for a drink. The hotel was still closed for the winter but Mary let me in and took me to the bar and served me. I know her now for her great kindness, but she can be dour dour. Her brother is Neil MacDonald, direct in line from Somerled, through Alastair MacIan who was murdered in Glencoe in 1693. He is Neil MacDonald of MacDonald of Glencoe. He is a retired forester, and shepherd. Some retirement! He is at the lambing outside the window as I write. Muttering something about getting the owner, Mary left me in the bar to sip my drink. I was still sleekit like a wet rat, and the crutch-piece of my wet suit was unfastened and hung down behind me.

The owner came into the bar. She was Jeannette Stewart. I remember still how she stopped and stood by the door and looked at me. She stood with her back to the door, tall and dark and athletic, slim as a wand, looking at me in silence. I looked back. For a long time neither of us spoke.

A red haze came over my eyes, and there was shouting and roaring in my ears. I could have killed for her and still would.

I took a step forward. I wanted to say,

> *'It is the secret sympathy,*
> *The silver link, the silken tie,*
> *Which heart to heart, and mind to mind,*
> *In body and in soul can bind.'*

But all I could do was bow, and say, 'What'll ye have to drink?'

That was my first mistake. Jeannette asked for a glass of wine. I called for champagne. A quick fumble in my pocket told me I hadn't enough.

'Make it a half bottle,' I added, spoiling the grand gesture, and giving an impression of invincible meanness, which I am still teased about, but it was no time to go on the slate. Then I poured her a glass, and one for another lady who was in the bar. The rest I poured, still looking at her, into my pint of beer.

We fought. All that spring and into the summer we fought. Jeannette is gently bred. I am me. Jeannette speaks proper. I Paisley. Jeannette knows how to use a knife and fork, and thinks it important. I eat. Jeannette drinks wine. I bevvy. Jeannette's ears had occasionally been soiled by words which come readily to a soldier's tongue. I use them. So does Jeannette now. All that spring we fought and snarled like lovers. But it was a lovely fight. I was broke and she gave me money. I bought an old banger of a car, and when I closed the birthplace in the evenings I raced ten thousand miles across the winding roads of Scotland to be beside her. I raced back in dawns alive with birdsong, alive with my songs too. I pursued her until that summer she ran off to Canada to get away from me. She fled across the North American continent, pursued by a grapeshot of letters, telegrams, and phone calls. She hadn't a chance of escaping. Neither had I.

A year later, on 5 April 1974, we were married in Inveraray Registry office, two registrar's clerks acting as witnesses. We got into her car and drove towards Lochgilphead. For half an hour the silence was total. Finally I asked her what she was thinking.

The first words she spoke to me as my wife were, 'I'm appalled at what I've just done.'

I gave a great laugh and pulled the car into the side of the road and kissed her. After long travelling, I had come home again.

Sixteen years later Jeannette is still appalled at what she did that morning, but she is still my wife. She is in the next room as I write these lines. So is our son Stewart.

15 The Flying Advocate

YOU CANNOT SUPPORT a wife on a museum curator's salary, so I gave in my notice. Just before I left Kirrie, a circus came to town. They were looking for a barker. A barker goes ahead putting up playbills, and arranging publicity. At nights he stands at the door of the big-top and barks. It seemed to me that a Scottish advocate was well qualified for the job, and it paid handsomely. A bit of haggling with the owner, who was also the strong-man and the mule trainer, got me the candy-floss concession as a bonus. I suggested to Jeannette that travelling the summer roads of Scotland with a circus would make an ideal honeymoon but she put her foot down. Always biddable, I did what I was told, and we set up our married life together in the Falls of Lora Hotel.

But what to do? Hotel life held no interest for me, and I was not going to be a gofer for my wife, a kept man. Jeannette owned half a small farm. Long ago the farm had provided a living for a family, but these days were past. Intensive small scale vegetable growing seemed a possibility. No one had ever grown vegetables on a commercial scale in the West Highlands, and The Highlands and Islands Development Board were interested. So were the bank. They each put up half the capital I needed, particularly since I was willing to work for a starvation wage.

It is always possible to start from nothing. Circumstances have forced me to do it so many times that it comes naturally. I spent a lot of time learning this new trade from books, and on several intensive weekends at the Agricultural College. Things grew for me. I had sixteen acres under vegetables, and it is relentless savage work. For five years I ploughed the fields and scattered. There was great happiness in it, but very little money, and when our son Stewart was born in October 1975 I knew I would have to try to make more.

I still had many friends in law, but it seemed impossible to make a comeback. That life had been frittered away. My old friend Bill Dunlop, one of the great fierce characters which Scots law shapes for its own ends, was keen for me to take a case in the High Court, and so was his partner Morris Smythe. I agreed, and a long-suffering Faculty of Advocates let me back in. I always resigned from the Faculty when I went walkabout. This permitted me to moonlight as a solicitor's clerk doing conveyancing to supplement whatever pittance I was earning. I tried to do things the proper way by resigning from the Faculty before I went moonlighting, but you are not really supposed to behave like that. You are supposed to treat advocacy as a career, not as a convenience. On my return I found things had changed. No longer was it necessary to live in Edinburgh, and life broadened out for me, one day on my tractor, the next day in court. It was a strange mixture, and aeroplanes made it even stranger.

Aeroplanes have always been one of my true loves, and I had taken a licence away back in the 1960s. To roll off the top of a loop, when the straps suddenly hit your shoulders, and the whole sky revolves round you, brings a serenity which has no parallel. Serenity is a chosen word. I have sat beside other pilots watching their face, and at the moment when hands and feet and eye are all in co-ordination the sweetness of absolute control brings a fine thin smile to the face. The Oban bank manager was easily persuaded that there should be an aeroplane for hire on the airstrip at North Connel, and I went into the aircraft hire business. Sadly my first aeroplane Tango November was lost on Mull, causing the death of the pilot, Peter Gibbs, and creating what is still known as the Great Mull Air Mystery.

Peter Gibbs was a stranger to me when he came to hire Tango November just before Christmas 1975. He had flown fighters during the war and was a pilot of some experience and great daring. His daring cost him his life. After dinner on

Christmas Eve, in a blink between heavy rain squalls, he took off from the airstrip at Glen Forsa on Mull to do a circuit of the airfield. There are no lights whatever on Glen Forsa, and no radio. It was a flight of the most utter foolhardiness. Tango November's navigation lights were last seen apparently approaching the airstrip over the sea from the east. They disappeared behind some trees, and vanished. Despite an intensive air, sea, and mountain search nothing was found. No debris on sea or land. Nothing. Here was a mystery.

The mystery was compounded when the body of Peter Gibbs was found by a shepherd in March. He was sitting propped in the fork of a fallen tree, five hundred feet up on a hill overlooking the airstrip. His body was quite undamaged, and he had died from exposure. Years later clam divers found Tango November on the seabed, not far from the end of the airstrip. A reconstruction of the occurrence suggests that the unfortunate pilot, realising it was impossible ever to find an unlit airfield in these foul weather conditions, ditched along the line of the breakers, and waded ashore. In the intense darkness, which only a countryman can appreciate, he walked across the road and climbed the hill to try to get his bearings. When he sat down on a tree to rest he was done for. You die very quickly on a highland hill in December. He lies in Pennyfuir cemetry, and occasionally I go there to try to purge myself of my unworthy feelings. At the time my feeling was not grief for a lost life, but fury for the loss of a much-loved aeroplane.

Other aeroplanes succeeded Tango November, but none was more loved. I eked out a precarious existence as an owner-pilot. Precarious because the bank was the true owner of all my aircraft, and somehow they had to be made to pay. For two years I was chief pilot to the Scottish Parachute Club at Auchterarder, often sleeping in flying overalls and a polythene bag under the wing of my aircraft, one of life's great experiences. In my flying career I wrote off two aircraft; one through carelessness; one through weather. In Scotland the weather is never safe for flying, yet those days when I flew from Connel to Glasgow in time to change from flying overalls to wig and gown are among the happiest in my life. I was always broke, and there was always just enough money for fuel, yet seeing Scotland from the air added another dimension to my love.

My return to the Bar turned me into a jury lawyer. In my earlier days all my work had been civil. I had considered it a bonus when I crept away from the Parliament House, to the annoyance of my clerk, to take a criminal trial, which in these days was quite unpaid. Now on my return it was jury trial after jury trial, and all cases were fee-ed by the Legal Aid Board. In Scotland the fees for criminal work are minimal, and they have never kept step with the rise in travelling costs and hotel bills. They are paid a year or more after the work is finished, by which time they are devalued, by inflation, and by interest rates. No one gets rich. Of all legal work it is however the most satisfying. In civil work you fight for money and property, usually for people who can afford to lose. In criminal work you fight for liberty, and your client stands to lose everything. On the brief words of a jury verdict he walks out into the sunlight, or down into a cell. Until the words of the verdict are spoken, you never know which it is to be. A fight for liberty is the noblest fight of all. Such work has brought me great happiness and satisfaction, if a lesser financial reward. Gradually I ran down the market garden, until I was back full time as an advocate.

In 1980 the Queen appointed me to the rank and dignity of a Queen's Counsel of Scotland. It is the only rank and dignity I have ever aspired to and I am very proud of it. Proud but not pompous. The Scot hates pomposity, and I still attend court in an anorak, and on cold days a woollen bunnet. The longer I practise as an advocate the more humble it makes me. To have the privilege of addressing the highest court of your country should make any man feel humble, and the experience of being an aircraftsman second class, and all the other humble jobs I have done has bred in me a great feeling of respect for those who bear the burden of high judicial office, as well as for the inarticulate people who appear before them. That may not be entirely apparent from these pages, but it is apparent in every one of my court appearances. I can fight with a judge just as easily as anyone else, but there are other more subtle ways of pleading, and the longer I am at the job the more I turn to such ways. The High Court could have claimed me for ever had it not been for my itchy feet, and a sudden feeling of disgust with Scotland.

In 1979 the Labour Government held a plebiscite in Scotland in which a majority of Scots voted for some form of self-government, but nothing came of it. The Labour Party in Scotland were against it openly and covertly. No doubt the faithful labour stalwarts wished always to have the lush pastures of Westminster to graze in. That is all Parliament is to the Labour Party; a reward for services, rather than a place to serve. I challenge any reader of this book to name any ten Scottish Labour Members of Parliament. They are more anonymous than sheep. The Tories are worse. They are plain treacherous. Lord Home of the Hirsel said 'Trust me. This Home Rule Bill is a bad one. Vote against it and I will use all my personal influence to bring in a better one.' He never did, yet this quisling is regarded by the Tories as one of their great elder statesmen. We sold the hotel, and like Fletcher of Saltoun shook the dust of Scotland from our feet and emigrated, leaving a country fit only for the slaves who had betrayed it.

Of course it was a mistake. I went ahead of Jeannette to become an articled law clerk in Medicine Hat in Alberta. It was a fine clear autumn day in 1980. As the aircraft passed over Kintyre, and the Mull of Oa of Islay I looked down from my seat, and tried to pretend that I was leaving all this for ever. We would change utterly. We would hunt the dollar. We were going out to a secure job, in a secure and well-governed country. All I had to do was to pass seventeen exams in one year and we would be set up for life, and rich. Our son would never feel the aching of unrequited love for his country that his father has always suffered.

I passed the seventeen exams, although it took me fifteen months, not twelve. The workload was very heavy, as I had to earn a living during the day. I was permitted to appear in the Albertan equivalent of the Sheriff Court, and if a Scottish silk cannot outshine the lawyers of a Canadian province, he should not wear silk. I was never short of clients and I earned my salary. Nothing changed my love for Scotland. It still ached. I know now that it is with me until I die, and if there is an after-life to beyond. Nor did it make us rich. Half way through our time in Medicine Hat the bottom fell out of the oil market, and Alberta relied heavily on oil for its prosperity. The house we had bought became scarcely saleable, and on the advice of the bank we had put the proceeds of the hotel into 'Blue Chip' shares. They were oil shares, and overnight they fell to a quarter of their value. All that was left was sufficient to cover the balance of the mortgage on the house. Broke but determined, we knew we had to get back to Scotland.

First I had to go to Calgary to sell my aeroplane, or rather the bank's aeroplane. In Canada aeroplanes were used almost as cars, and I put in several hundred hours flying, having several snarls with air traffic controllers, who are a fascist breed to us free pilots. They did for me in the end, but it was a fitting end, both to my flying career, and to my career as a Canadian lawyer.

The City of Calgary is named after a beach on the Isle of Mull. It is a fine city, overlooked at a distance by the Rocky Mountains. Having made all the necessary arrangements to sell my aeroplane I set out to pilot myself back to Medicine Hat. I knew it would be my last flight. Shortly we would return to Scotland, where I would have to start from scratch again and work hard. There would be no money for flying. Also most pilots as they get older get more and more careful, but this had not happened to me, and if I did not stop, my blood was soon going to mix with the instruments. I was determined that my last flight would be a memorable one.

I took off from Calgary Springfield on the last day of March 1982, and headed for the Rocky Mountains. In flying you hang in the air utterly relaxed, and the steady drone of the engine is like silence. I climbed towards the mountains, determined to do some high flying, and some low flying on this, my last flight. It is forbidden in Canada to fly above ten thousand feet, but close in to the mountains I thought they would not get me on their radar screen. I flew very close. I had a poor opinion of Canadian radio and radar. They could never get me when I wanted a fix, and they were great natterers on the radio, which I now switched off. I was alone in the sky, alone in a very powerful aeroplane. A great mountain peak loomed above me. I opened the throttle, and fined the pitch. We soared in the turbulent air of the peak, buffetting and plunging in its down-wind plume. I had left the warm cabin of my Cessna. I was now Group Captain, the Duke of Hamilton on his first epic flight in an open cockpit aeroplane over Everest. My goggles froze to my face as I fought with the controls. It was tough.

Far far below me and to the east I saw a lake. I laid the aircraft on its side, and kicked on bottom rudder. We dropped out of the sky, all the dials shuddering in the red, the whole kite screaming. There was a sound of rice falling on a tin tray as I pulled out above the surface of the lake. That was the rivets popping out the wings. I was now Group Captain Leonard Cheshire VC terror of the Mohne. I hummed the theme music from the Dambusters as I flew among the great black balls of evil flack. The dam wall appeared before me, grey and stretching to the sky, higher than a house. A great heave on the controls and we cleared it by inches. The white startled face of a technician appeared at a door, a wing-breadth away. The whole fuselage shook as my rear-gunner scythed him to pieces. One boche down; forty-five million to go. Skeeeeeer. Splaaaaaaat. The dam was bust.

I put the nose down and sped at roof-top level or below over the flat fields of France. I was now Wing Commander Douglas Bader, DSO DFC and Bar, looking for targets of opportunity. Keraaaaaaaah. Bang. What's that on the end of the Pitot tube? Ah. Only the head of a Hun motor cyclist. Nothing in that.

I pulled up to about fifty feet and crept away. I was now Ian Hamilton, exhilarated but feeling rather ashamed of myself. A few telephones would be ringing. Better to keep under the radar screen for half an hour and approach Medicine Hat from the other side. In a flight like this, which I see from my log-book took three hours twenty minutes, you keep a running plot in your head of where you are, and sure enough Medicine Hat turned up as expected. I joined the circuit, did my checks and prepared to land. As I came on close finals I noticed three police cars and an ambulance parked outside the hangar. Had there been an accident?

Every pilot makes his last landing. Too many of my friends have made theirs in a cloud-wrapped hill, or at night, lost and out of fuel. I was luckier. Mine was a good one and I taxied in. But what about these police cars? What about the ambulance? Naive as it sounds it never occurred to me that they were for me. Wherever I had done my low flying I had been careful to come down out of the sun, and while I was sure they would be looking for me, sure also that I would have to return some bland answers and give some blank stares, I did not expect a reception committee. Canadian radar could not be all that hot.

I was soon disabused. I closed the engine down, and as soon as the propeller kicked to a stop two monstrous-sized policemen dragged me from the aeroplane and I was carried away between them, like a protest in parenthesis. The police car did not stop until it reached Medicine Hat police station. A cell door gives an awfully dull thud when it closes on you. I was in the slammer.

Not many lawyers have had that experience, and those who have are usually there for an over-exuberance with their client's money. Sitting in the cell, which smelled as all cells do of vomit, urine, and disinfectant, I reflected wryly that if I had flown like that in my teens, nobody would have made a fuss about it. I might even have got promotion. An hour or two later they needed the cell for a more demanding sort of person, and I was let out. Canadians are wonderful people. They make stern laws, and like the Scots they go ahead and break them. I knew all the police in that station by name, many of them by their first name. Their treatment of me, once an early indignation had passed, was beyond reproach. Their attitude was one of admiration for what they thought I had done, mixed with sorrow that I had been caught. My old enemies, the air traffic controllers had had me on radar all the time, and were far from pleased. Before I left the police station I had to surrender my log-book, and pilot's licence. I have retrieved my log-book, but I have never flown again.

Flying infringements are a federal offence in Canada, and are prosecuted from an office in far-away Ottawa. If they were going to do anything other than forfeit my licence it would take a week or two to do it. I had no great curiosity to wait and see. I had made many friends in Medicine Hat. One was a self-made millionaire, and what a gentle humble fellow he was. He was also a pilot of many thousands of hours of experience. To him I was something of a hero. I had done something he had always wanted to do, or perhaps had already done without being caught. Anyway he was a shoulder to weep on. He was also a hand to help. A night or two later I packed two suitcases into his car and he drove me to Calgary International. Farewell Canada. Poor Jeannette was left to wind up all our affairs in Medicine Hat.

The plane from Calgary stopped to refuel at Goose Bay or

Gander. I forget which. I was paying no attention. I had the hunted feeling of an escaping felon. The whites of my eyes showed at every approaching footstep. When we were airborne again I could not even muster a weak smile for the air hostess until we were abeam Cape Farewell in Greenland, too far out for the pilot to put back should he get the radio call to 'bring back Ian Hamilton', which my guilty conscience felt was sure to come.

The Canadian interlude, like so many in my life was a pleasant one to look back on, particularly the closing event. I never had any trouble in the practice of the law. I had no difficulty in holding my own against practitioners of some repute who had spent a lifetime under the Canadian discipline. A few hours in a law library acquainted me with the basics of their law, which is founded on the English system, and is very different from Scots law. A lawyer however is a lawyer, anywhere in the world. He is trained to have an agility of mind, and to know what the law ought to be. A quick reference to a book will inform him whether or not he is right, and he should seldom find himself at a loss. In Canada there is no formal division of the profession as there is at home. But in fact the profession divides itself to the great detriment of the service it gives to the public. The large firms in the larger cities have chambers lawyers and court lawyers in their partnerships. This gives them the power to gain a monopoly of the richest clients, and they have little time for the small man. The country practitioner is not specialist enough to cover all the fields of human frailty and greed, and there is no Bar to turn to for advice. The wide training I had had as a Scottish advocate stood me in great stead.

Canadian lawyers are not very good. They get a very thorough training in law, but in nothing else. The nobbiest University is Osgoode Law School in Ontario. It turns out practitioners who know everything about law, and nothing about life. A Canadian lawyer can give you all the right answers to the questions he knows, but a lawyer has to know the answers to the unexpected, and that is where they fail. Drop a mention of a statute like the Miscellaneous Provisions and Family Planning Act of 1974, and they will spend eye-glazing hours trying to find it. They never will. I've just invented it. No Scots lawyer would fall for a trick like that. With no training in any other discipline than the law, they never seemed to be able to twist and change the presentation of their argument to meet the changing nuances of the court. Also they leave their sense of humour at the door of the courtroom, and the dry quip, usually made against oneself or the whole community, and so much loved by the Bench, is seldom heard in Canada.

One day Darwin Greaves, the agent for the Attorney General in South Alberta, and the only really able pleader I met, was vigorously opposing bail for my client, on the grounds that he was a transient who lived in a tent, a very cogent reason.

Very much tongue in cheek I answered that this was a plea that I had never expected to be advanced in a town like Medicine Hat.

'Until very recently,' I observed, 'all the best people in Alberta lived in tents.' There was a gasp in court and Darwin shot me a look of fury, but I knew my judge. He was a young Austrian immigrant, still with a thick accent, and I could see his suppressed laughter as he granted my client bail.

But perhaps my abiding memory is sweating and studying for those seventeen examinations. The examiners expected the candidates to have memorised great screeds of statute law, which I duly did. I never saw the purpose of it when it could all be found without too much sweat in any law library. However I duly passed all the examinations, and was called to the Canadian Bar, or more correctly to the Albertan Bar. And muckle good did it dae me.

What a relief it was to be back home. I borrowed a map of the world and scored off Canada. That makes two countries I can't return to.

16 Two Final Follies

ONCE AGAIN it seemed I had only been away on a short holiday. Work came to me. We rented a house near Bannockburn, and when we had scraped a few pennies together, bought one in Dollar, that lovely little hill-foot town beneath the Ochils. Stewart went to Dollar Academy, once one of Scotland's foremost schools. We liked living in Dollar, and I commuted from there to court, but ever our hearts turned towards Argyll, that enduring heartland of ancient Scotland. Heartland it is indeed. Argyll is a corruption of *Ard Gael*, the shore of the Gael.

Our worry was Stewart's education. Jamie, my other son had stayed with us and gone to Oban High. It had been a great school when Jamie was there. But one of its former teachers was John MacKay, once one of the Tory manikins in St Andrew's House, and for a short time MP for Argyll. As a result Oban High had been targetted by the teachers' unions for their strike action, and it seemed to us that the school might be demoralised. We did not want to send Stewart away, if he could get a good education while staying at home. Once, not so long ago, Scottish education was the best in the world. For twenty-five years successive governments have gone against the whole grain of our country and spent less and less on education, until teachers are now wretchedly under-paid, and public education is done on the cheap. In these circumstances my course as a parent is simple. If there is not enough in the educational trough for all, me and mine will eat first. I do not believe in private education, but if it is the best, then I will have it. The problem was solved for us by the Rector of Dollar Academy.

Dollar was largely populated by executives from mulit-nationals at places like Grangemouth. Fine fellows they were, but we did not want our son to grow up like them. No

Scot should be bred to be someone's lackey, however well paid. One day at some festival of the school, Easter, or Christmas, or the summer holidays the Rector was telling us how good Dollar Academy was.

'I have been speaking to someone high up in ICI', he said with pride, 'and he tells me that the Dollar product is just what ICI wants'.

I stamped my feet in derision, to find that the other parents were stamping theirs in applause. That was the end. My children can choose whatever they want to do, but I will not have them bred to be capitalist fodder. We arranged for Stewart to go to Rannoch, a school where they train kids to be self-reliant, and to hell with these quaint ambitions of grooming them to make money for other people. Meantime we made plans to return to Argyll, and started thinking of building a house on Jeannette's wee bit of land there. Before returning to Argyll two acts of folly overwhelmed me. One was to cause me great frustration, the other nearly killed me. Both were self-inflicted.

The first act of folly was to take a sheriffdom. It was springtime, 1985, and I had had a long hard winter in the courts, driving home in the dark every night. It seemed to me that the rest of my life should be spent in a relaxed fragrance, administering justice, and playing golf. What rubbish. Golf infuriated me. It is harder than it looks, and I never took to it. It is all right if you don't count the strokes. Sheriffing I found equally frustrating. I was appointed a sheriff of Strathkelvin and Strathclyde, at Glasgow, and while I enjoyed sitting on the Bench, I always felt out of place. It is a somewhat tame job after the excitement of the High Court, and although I bought a powerful motorbike, and commuted to court on it I never took to sheriffing. I believe I carried myself well, and did a proper job, but a sheriff spends long hours in his side-room waiting for things to happen, and I did not find this easy to cope with. To ease the boredom I took three canaries in to work in a cage, and they sang to me during the tedious hours.

It was during the miners' strike, and I got them by chance from a lachrymose pitman in a pub.

'See these little dears', he said to me. 'They would sing to break your heart, the little darlings'.

I peered at them through the bars of their cage. Right enough, they were singing away merrily as though they were as fu' as their owner.

'And what will happen to them?' he asked rhetorically.

If this strike doesn't end, the cat will get them'.

No man of feeling could resist such a plea, so I bought them. My arrival home with three canaries in a cage did not please Jeannette. She told me to take them right back where I got them, or they would go in to work with me next morning, so to work they went. They were a great solace.

After two months as a sheriff I realised that the job was not for me. The thought that I would be doing this until the long chimney of the crematorium crept above the horizon dismayed me, and I went to see the Sheriff Principal. He was John Dick, and he could not have been more kind. No one had ever resigned voluntarily from the Sherival Bench before, and I did not want to bring that high office into disrepute. There was much coming and going with the civil servants of the Scottish Courts Administration, and I agreed to continue to sit for some time after my resignation as a temporary sheriff, but even then it took me until December 1985 to disengage myself.

The other act of folly was in fulfillment of a boyhood ambition. Round about 1937 Penguin Books published an account of one of the first solo transatlantic crossings under sail. It is called *The Fight of the Firecrest,* by Alain Gerbault, and it is one of the great classics of sail. It fired a boyhood ambition in me, which grumbled away and sometimes came back to haunt me. As a young man I had sailed small boats with my friend Norman Wylie, now Lord Wylie, but I had never sailed a yacht. Back at the Bar things were going quite well for us, when one evening I was mooning about the house, discontented when I had no right to be.

Out of the blue Jeannette said, 'Why don't you buy a boat?'

These are the only foolish words that wise wise woman has uttered in sixteen years of marriage. I went on the hunt.

I knew what I wanted. It must be a wooden boat, because plastic boats are made without love for yuppies. It must sail straight up and down, and not on its side, because a leaning-over boat frightens me. It must be at least thirty feet long, because anything less would be too uncomfortable on a long passage, and the passage to the Carribean and back is seven thousand miles. I intended to do it in my summer holidays with only one stop. There are many reasons for nurturing a boyhood ambition. Mine was to see what it was like out there, and to see what I was like out there. Every adventure is a voyage of discovery into yourself.

I found *Aiva* at Craobh Haven. She was forlorn and dirty; ill-kempt; untended. But she was proud and confident in her beauty. She was twenty-seven feet long, a trifle small for what I had in mind. The cockpit was in the middle, and there was a little cabin behind, the back-bedroom as it was immediately called. Down three steps was the main cabin. It had two bunks, a kitchen and a lavatory. *Aiva* was a two room and kitchen afloat. I bought her for five thousand pounds.

Five thousand pounds was only the start. Madness then set in, because nothing was too good for *Aiva*. Buy a wooden boat and you are one with Ulysses. There is a benediction in a wooden boat. Men with skills now dead wrought her. She grew under their hands in a cradle, a love-child of many craftsmen. She was twenty-three years of age, and I found out later that she had been designed by Angus Primrose, one of the last great designers of wooden boats. Indeed he had disappeared on her sister-ship on a solo voyage to the Azores. He was an old man and it is a good way to go. All that remained was to learn to sail.

My son Jamie taught me. He had never sailed a yacht either, but he very quckly found out what all the ropes and things were for, and by watching him, I learned also. In all our spare time during the summer of 1986 we sailed her about the Clyde, round the Mull of Kintyre and out to the Western Isles. It was all horrible. Sailing is wet, cold, dangerous, expensive, and it gives you no exercise at all. All it gives you is seasickness and piles, these and a deadly fear. We persevered. We had both sea-fever, but it became clear that for an Atlantic passage a great deal still needed to be done to *Aiva*.

It was done that winter by Aron Bose of the Kyles of Bute Boatyard. Aron is a strange quiet man. He crewed John Ridgeway on one of the Whitbread round the world races, and is himself an ocean sailor of great experience. To Aron I took *Aiva* in December 1986. I told him my intentions, and what I wanted done to my boat. I did not tell him I had only been sailing for one season. He gave me some estimates, and they staggered me.

I was then sixty-one years of age. If anyone thinks that is too old, let him read Tennyson's *Ulysses*. If that is your age, you will never go adventuring younger. It was then or never, and money is useless to you on the Atlantic Ocean. People don't do things because they can afford to. They do things because they want to. Indeed most rich people don't do very much at all. They cross the Atlantic by Concorde, not in an old twenty-seven foot boat. I bit on it and got a personal loan for £5000. I'm still paying it back. That was not enough. Even yet I have not totalled what it cost to fit-out *Aiva*, but it must have been in excess of £15000.

Sea-fever is insidious. It does not take away your wits, only your judgment. It narrowly focusses your vision. Nothing else is important, only getting to sea. All that winter I studied charts and navigation. I taught myself to use a sextant, and although I could not understand spherical trigonometry, I reckoned that America was such a big target that even I could not miss it. My sea plan depended on weather plots. I had to get into and out of the Carribean before the hurricane season began in late June. This meant an April start from the Clyde, and a sprint under the engine for Finisterre, south of which I would pick up the Portuguese Trade Winds, edging westwards all the time. A thirty-five day passage should see me to English Harbour Antigua. *Aiva* had fuel for eight hundred miles, and that was ample to see me through the Doldrums. I would refuel and revictual at English Harbour, set off northwards towards Bermuda, catch the westerlies and the Gulf Stream, and be back in court in seventy days to start earning money to pay off all these debts. Let people laugh. At least I tried. But so much depended on the weather.

You might as well consult the entrails of a dead hen as consult weather men. But on 16 April 1987 they told me that there was a window opening in the weather that should get me from the Clyde across Biscay, and maybe even down into the Trades. The entry for the following day on *Aiva's* log reads.

> This day *Aiva* is cleared by UK Port Authorities
> for English Harbour, Antigua and Barbuda. Master,
> Ian Robertson Hamilton, Queen's Counsel, 54 High
> Street, Dollar. No other crew. No passengers.

Who was kidding whom? *Aiva* was still on the slip.

That day was frenetic, but finally about noon Aron climbed up the cradle to *Aiva's* little aft deck. We shook hands in silence, and he left me alone. The trolley rattled down the rails, Aiva bowed and curtseyed her way into the sea, and I started the engine and set course for America.

The first thing to go wrong was a hundred yards from the slipway. *Aiva* started to go round in circles. I had left the vane self-steering unlocked. The vane self-steering is a device which operates a second rudder when under sail to steer *Aiva* slantwise across the wind. A nail from the pocket of my oilskins did the trick, and again we were under-way. Then the electric self-steering fused, and had to be repaired with sticky tape. By this time we were abeam Tighnabruaich pier. We had still a long way to go to the Spanish Main.

The route to the Spanish Main from Tighnabruaich lies through the Kerry Kyle and down the Kilbrannan Sound. An oily April sea lapped the shores of the Kerry Kyle and *Aiva* left only a sullen wake. I adjusted the throttle for five knots, and brought her on to the correct compas course. I set to to secure stores, lash things in position, and trim ship. That done, the next job was to get the sails out. Bending on a mainsail is not a difficult job in a dockyard, but even then it takes time. At sea it takes longer. A well found boat can sail happily without the skipper's hand on the tiller, and can just as happily run itself aground if he is doing something else. The grey skies cupped their hands together and closed in round *Aiva*, and took the shore away. I had to keep watch. There was no chance now to bend on the sail. In these conditions I could not leave the tiller. We pressed on towards nightfall.

Night found us south of Arran entering the North Channel. Making a passage at night is easier than by day. The light houses guide you. The lights on the Galloway shore came up to port, passed abeam, and dropped astern. We entered the darkness of the Irish Sea. The sea began to get rough. *Aiva* rose and crashed down on the short, tidal breaking waves. The skipper was sick. You vomit on to your down-wind shoulder and get on with it, and you never feel lonely. You are never alone with a boat.

Dawn broke with a heavy sea and an uneasy wind. It came in great puffs, as though blowing at a candle. In the Irish Sea the waves do not come in the long rolling pattern you get in the Atlantic. They come in great lumps and hit you like concrete. Among the repairs the yard had done were repairs to the very bottom of the hull. If they were not sound we would go to the bottom in a gulp. Jonah had faith in the Maker of the whale, I in Aron Bose. But it was time to listen to the radio, and find out what had happened to the good weather the Met men had talked about. The barometer was dropping like a stone.

'Security. Security. Security.' These are the words that the coastguards use to preface bad news. It was bad indeed. 'Sea areas Lundy, Fastnet, Irish Sea. Southerly Gale imminent.' I was in trouble.

Trouble in the Irish Sea is trouble indeed. South of Belfast Lough there is no deep water harbour. Or none that I had the confidence to try to make. The entrances are shallow, and in a gale the waves, forced upwards by the shallowness of the seabed, break in great crests. More sailors are drowned trying to make port than are drowned at sea. I decided to try to ride it out. From the cockpit there was only a wastey wilderness of lumpy water. A great grey widow-maker of a sea crashed by, taking the vane of the self-steering gear with it, but Aiva shipped not one sea in the cockpit, and I carried a spare vane. I went below and listened to the radio. One by one the fishing boats at sea were reporting to the coastguard that they had reached harbour. I had not let the coastguards know I was at sea. I don't like Big Brother watching me, and I had every confidence in my dead-reckoning position.

My dead-reckoning position put me fifteen miles south-west of the Calf of Man. If we kept going southwards under a trickle of power, we would get into wider seas and ride it out. At worst we could run before the gale under a bare mast, back through the North Channel to the Clyde. But I was tired. The vomiting had stopped but I had been in the cockpit now for twenty-six hours, and awake for a lot longer than that. I was also weak. I had not gone into physical training for the trip, and courts make you soft. It was time to get some kip. I went below and jammed myself into my bunk, with my right shoulder under the bookshelf, and my left hand curled round the bottom of the bunk, and went to sleep.

Sleep was shattered by a grounching noise coming from the engine, and wakefulness brought home that my left wrist was wet, and that my left hand was under water. Aiva was sinking. I went into the cockpit, and stopped the engine, and switched on the electric bilge pump, and manned the hand-pump, and the level of the water rapidly went down. *Aiva* is a small boat, and these were big pumps. But if the engine wasn't running how long would the batteries last to run the electric pump, and how long would my strength last to man the hand one? And where was the leak? Where was the water coming from? This was an inauspicious start to an ocean passage.

Clearly we must stop and start again. But where to go? All the old arguments about making port still applied. The nearest harbours were Port Erin or Port St Mary, in the Isle of Man, but both were open to the south where the gale was still to come from. It was time to call the coastguard as the fishing boats had done, and say that I was leaking and making for Port Erin. Would they keep a look-out for me, and advise me how to get behind the harbour wall? The coastguard took a grimmer view of the situation and called out the Port Erin lifeboat.

The lifeboat searched for me all afternoon, and found me seventeen miles south west of the Calf of Man, just as dusk was falling. A small boat is almost invisible in a broken sea, and I was spotted by a brave lifeboatman who spent the entire search in the bow of the lifeboat. He was alternately raised high in the air, and plunged into the green seas. One incident nearly did for me. I was asked by the cox, with whom I was in radio contact, to fire a flare. A flare sends successive balls of fire a thousand feet into the air. What the books don't tell you is the obvious thing that when you fire it, it kicks like a pistol. When you need a flare most you are too stupid with tiredness to work that out for yourself. When it kicked it kicked out of my hand, and fell in the cockpit, and spat violent balls of fire at the aft bulkhead. The scar on *Aiva's* woodwork is still there. If the flare had pointed the other way the balls of fire would have hit me where I stood in the companionway. They might have killed me. Tired as I was, I got the microphone out with one hand and the fire extinguisher with the other. For the first, and I hope the last time in my life, I put out a Mayday. But the extinguisher worked, and I stood down the Mayday.

Maydays are the day-to-day work of lifeboatmen. I am stunned with admiration for these men. Yet that was not my feeling when they discovered me in the Irish Sea. Would that it had been anybody but me! I am by nature a rescuer, not a casualty. I resented it. You have all seen pictures of lifeboats with lifeboatmen in their yellow life-jackets lining the rails. There is no need to put to sea and be rescued, just to see that. The picture conveys the reality. But you must put to sea and be rescued to know the rage, the resentment, and the shame. People who go alone to sea, or into the hills, should rely only on themselves, not on others. I bitterly regret that call to the coastguard. It was advisory only, not asking for help. I might have made it on my own, with a little advice over the radio. Yet if I detach myself from my own feelings, how much I admire the warm calmness of both the coastguards, and of the lifeboatmen. There was not a word of reproach in them.

I told the lifeboatmen that I would open the sea-cocks and sink *Aiva*. They had done enough, and the wind was freshening. Besides I was exhausted, and could scarcely stand up. My strength would not last to con *Aiva* on a long and difficult tow, but lifeboatmen are made of steadier stuff than lawyers. They would have none of it. They would bring *Aiva* safe to port, and they did. They took me aboard the lifeboat and I lay in the fo'c'sle with one of the lifeboatmen who had cracked two ribs when he was flung across the wheelhouse by a sea. All I could contribute to that eight-hour tow was to piss in a sea-boot. There are no potties on a lifeboat.

They took me to hospital with the lifeboatman. I shouted my thanks from a stretcher. I was too weak to protest, and to be truthful, there was something comfortable in being looked after. Next morning, after the nurses assured me that the lifeboatman was recovering, I discharged myself, and took a taxi to the harbour. I had left Scotland with only a few shivering daffodils to show that spring was here, but in the Isle of Man the hawthorn was out. The wind had dropped. *Aiva* rode serenely at a buoy, and seemed to have stopped taking water. It was all a world away from a gale at sea. A few days passed before my strength returned, but I had to get *Aiva* to the yard up the coast at Peel. There was a lot of damage to the standing rigging, and the leak had to be investigated before I put to sea again. When *Aiva* was dried out against the harbour wall at Peel, we found a large polythene bag, the type used to contain farm fertiliser. It was wrapped round the propeller shaft. This had sprung the gland where the shaft goes through the hull, letting the water in. That was all. Just bad luck.

Repairs to *Aiva* had to wait for various parts. I lingered for some days, but it became obvious that there was no hope of an Atlantic crossing that year. I left Peel with reluctance. Peel is lovely. So is the Isle of Man. It once belonged to Scotland, and the locals are part Scots part Norse. They treated me with great kindness, and gradually my self-confidence returned. Then I flew home.

On the afternoon of my return home my eleven year old son Stewart came in. We looked at each other, then I said,

'I hope your friends are not giving you stick for having a father who set out for America and only reached the Isle of Man.'

Slender, clear-skinned, and calm-eyed, he replied, 'You got further than most people, Dad.'

Forgive a father's pride in that proud proud answer.

Next year was more sensible. Not America, but the Azores. The Azores are halfway from the Clyde to the Carribean, fifteen hundred nautical miles from Largs, or seventeen hundred road miles, only there is no road. Jamie came with me, and we left on 10 June 1988, a more benign time of the year than April. Last year's experience had been partly learned. *Aiva* was tested and in all respects ready for sea. The skipper was the weak link. The day before we left I had addressed a jury in Glasgow High Court, listened to the judge's charge, and left my junior to take the verdict.

The deck log of that voyage tells all. We went round the Mull of Kintyre and straight out north-west by Malin Head, and then west for a hundred miles to reach the hundred fathom line. Beyond that the great seas roll with two miles or more between them, and upon them the winds make their own slight sea. On the right hand page of the deck log you record course, and distance-run, and information about the wind and sea, and your position. The left hand page is for sums.

The most important sum was done during a night watch somewhere south-west of southern Ireland. It was a long complicated sum. It was calculating how few pesetas I would take for *Aiva* when we reached the Azores. Common sense had broken through at last. What on earth were we doing out here? We had lives to live at home, interesting lives, full of friends, and laughter, and fine jobs. There were challenges to be taken up and problems to be solved, and here we were plowtering about in a boat in mid-ocean. When the dawn came up I went down to the cabin and saw Jamie's face. I could see that he had the same feelings as I had.

'It's all right, Jamie,' I said. 'We're flying home.'

It was the boredom which got to us most of all. Just sitting there plugging along, day after day, and nothing but sea. Certainly we crossed the Gulf Stream, and the sea at night turned green like liquid sapphire. When you pissed into it, it was like pissing precious stones. As the stream hit the water each drop jumped into a glittering green jewel. Then there were the dolphins. They came every now and again, great graceful sea torpedos, cavorting round us in joy. Joyfully there for quarter of an hour, and then away. Then a great whale came and played round us, a fin whale, twenty seven metres long by the book. I was petrified, but Jamie stood calmly photographing it as it swam lazily alongside, so near that you could see its twin blow-holes opening and shutting, like evil winking eyes. Then it went a distance away and swam back, sounding to pass its great grey-blue submarine length like an endless shadow just under our keel. It blew with a sigh, with the sound of a great lazy wave breaking up a shelving shore. Then it too left us alone.

It was not the loneliness which got to us. It was just boredom. The weather was not all that bad. Scotland basked in a ridge of high pressure, that ran from the Azores to Norway, but a ripple ran along it and we were always in that ripple. Only one night did we have a star to steer her by. You hold the star against the rigging, and that keeps you on course. When there is no star you are peering constantly into the compass, which swings backwards and forwards lazily through ten degrees each side of your course. I never took my oilskins off on the whole trip. Once a gale hit us. We lashed the helm over to work against a small storm jib, and took to our bunks. A lee cloth, a triangle of sail which runs from under your bunk to the ship's side holds you in your bunk. You go into a coma, and the noise and the motion is indescribable. But it passes. It was a northerly gale, and even hove to it bore us sixteen miles on our way. But oh the boredom, and the weakness.

The constant motion of a small boat is enervating, and I grew weaker and weaker. I had no sea-sickness, but I could not eat. I resigned command to Jamie, and logged that I had done so. I forced down a raw egg each day, and some dried fruit. Day after day it went on, and then one day we knew we should have raised Graciosa, the most Northerly Island of the Azores. The visibility was poor, but we knew that it was there. We stood off until nightfall, and then through the gloom, we saw the lighthouse flashing. As we got nearer the shore, the street lights became visible, and at dawn Jamie conned her under sail into the tight and rockbound little harbour of Santa Cruz de Graciosa, and we dropped anchor. We had let the batteries run flat and could not start the engine. We were eighteen days out of the Clyde.

When we left the Clyde I had a picture of myself striding ashore immaculate in whites, and indeed I had whites to change into, but I was too weak. I was happy to take to the dinghy in the clothes I had worn for the whole trip, and to lever myself up the slimy steps of the quay on my bum. I could not stand for many minutes. *Aiva's* position at anchor in the harbour was perilous. She would have to be brought alongside, but she had no power. Jamie's French, and someone's broken English summoned help in the form of a power-boat. It was cradled down the slip. I turned wearily to go back aboard to bring *Aiva* alongside the little harbour wall.

Jamie said, 'When will you learn, father that you are sixty-two and that there's another generation to do these things? I'll go.'

I did not resent it. I was glad, and indeed proud. It was Jamie's triumph. He had pulled me through, and it is fine to have a son like that. Danger shared has made us closer than ever. But I have felt, and always will feel that I failed myself on that trip.

Island people are kind, and the people of Santa Cruz de Graciosa are the kindest I have ever met. After a few days rest we took *Aiva* the further fifty miles to the marina at Horta, the yachting cross-roads of the world. To get there every yacht has done a sea trip of more than a thousand miles. In Horta we hired a skipper to sail *Aiva* back to the Clyde. We flew.

And that is how I was cured of sea-fever.

I swear I will never adventure again. I have bought a pair of carpet slippers, although they have not had much wear yet. We have built our house, and settled down beside a remote lochan in Argyll. Half a mile away there is the sighing of the sea, and beneath our windows the ghost of William Butler Yeats breathes across the lapping of loch waters.

Yet incidents have not quite finished with me. On Christmas Eve 1988 I was standing on a grassy bank by the side of a country road, watching my son ride his pony, a saintly husband and father, a model of perfection.

At that moment Almighty Zeus woke from his afternoon nap, brushed his silvery locks from his serene brow, and in the language of Eden and Olympus said to Gannymede,

'Ganny, gonna go doon the off licence and get us a can of nectar?'

'Aye. Sure. Nae bother,' said Gannymede.

'Naw. Naw,' said Almighty Zeus in sudden sorrow. 'Therr's Ian Hamilton coming the old onion. See's a thunderbolt, Ganny.'

Two seconds later a car mounted the green grassy bank and hurled me many feet into a bed of rocks and brambles. Later in the day the hospital discharged me, the doctor saying, 'That one will keep you off work for two months.'

'All the fools aren't lawyers,' I snarled. 'Plenty left to be doctors,' but the doctors were right.

Next day at home, I was assisted into an armchair, my leg was raised onto a coffee-table, and I was propped up with pillows. Greatest insult of all, a rug was wrapped round me. My language was awful.

That wise and gentle lady Jeannette tended me. When she had suffered my ill-temper to burn itself out, she brought pen and paper and laid them beside me.

'Why don't you write a book?' she suggested.

You can't swear at an angel, or not for long anyway.

I started to write. The book I wrote is called, *A Touch of Treason*.

17 The Future is Ours

JUST AS THIS BOOK was published I had my sixty-fifth birthday. (God Bless you, Mr Lloyd George. You done well with yon budget of yours. You've been a good man to me and mine.) Sixty-five is a nice round comfortable figure. I can end my autobiography at it. But it is only a pausing point. The youth of age now enters upon me. I have many years to go even to the menopause. And thanks to Lloyd George, for the first time in my life I will have a steady income. I am studying pension plans. I shall invest my pension for my old age.

Looking back on the years, which are never a long time away, only yesterday, there is no discernible pattern. This is as it should be. A moor is more interesting than a ladder, a mountain climbs higher than a stairway. Had I stuck to the path, I would be at the summit now, and what do you do then? Rest? I can't. Judge? Don't be daft. I lack judgment. Teach youngsters? What nonsense. The only youngsters worth teaching learn for themselves. The received wisdom of age is yesterday's thought. And if I were to try to teach the young, the other elders would gang up on me, and kill me. A man only sees the first, far, faint gleam of success, when he is given, not his painting in oils, but a glass of hemlock. It is the last and greatest accolade.

The sword of the accolade will never touch my shoulders. I'm more likely to get hemp in the neck. That brings a smile. I must be older than I thought. I must guard against complacency. It is a greater killer of the old than arteriosclerosis, and many people catch it in their thirties. Better as you age to look on your failures. It is not too late to try again.

I regard my greatest failure as the-might-have-been of the Stone of Destiny. No. Not that it is back in Westminster. Those people who are always asking me if it is 'the real one' are bores. They have missed the point. A flag is no more than the device that is on it, and there is no such thing as the real flag, separate from its device. So it is with the Stone. The device is in Westminster behind bars, and there it should remain, until we provide for the Lord Clashferns of this world, and for all the ability poured into the sand. That is the only importance of 'getting home rule'. To provide, not jobs for the boys, but offices for people of great talent. On that view Scotland has failed James MacKay more than James has failed Scotland. Scotland endures, with or without political institutions. Yet there is no place for the best of us to serve, except in England. There is no high office at all in Scotland. The Stone, in England, does very well. Better behind bars, reminding us of our present condition, than as an empty symbol like the crown in Edinburgh Castle, the oldest in the world yet it is never worn.

The-might-have-been of the Stone of Destiny is this. Having seen it once brought back to Scotland, and the acclaim that that caused, people thought it could only be of value as a symbol when it was once again returned. That is not so at all. I confess now to a secret longing that I had then and still have. That longing is to see it as an ambition of every young Scot to attempt to spend a night's vigil before the Stone, like the vigil of the knight before the altar. It would also, for each individual, be his personal affront to the foreign government of Scotland, and an affirmation of his faith in the future of his country. He would be arrested, I expect, and charged with disorderly behaviour. I deny the right of any English court to punish any Scot for attempting to dedicate his life before the talisman of his people. I believe that the Community of the Realm of Scotland agrees with that. Not one Scot, not even Malcolm Rifkind, would want to see a young Scot punished for so conducting himself. All it needs is one youngster who is not afraid of being laughed at to start it. Others would follow. It would be a badge of merit to any employer, that the youngster had on his curriculum vitae. 'Did my time at Westminster'.

Such gestures are symbolic only, but I have this to say to young Scotland, 'Remember Mahatma Gandhi'. When he sought to overthrow British rule in India he turned not to violence but to salt. With a poke of salt Mahatma Gandhi freed a whole sub-continent. The British Government claimed to have a monopoly of salt, so Gandhi distilled a poke of salt from sea-water and carried it with him everywhere, even to the vice-regal lodge. It was his symbol of defiance. I clutch my poke of salt for Scotland. Yet I feel that I did not arouse people enough in my youth, that no salt has been spilled on the floor of Westminster Abbey. Spilt salt is a far more enduring symbol than spilt blood. And it causes fewer tears.

There are other uses for pokes of salt. When Lord President Cooper said that the doctrine of the sovereignty of Parliament had no place in the law of Scotland, no doubt it was the law of desuetude he had in mind. By that doctrine a law ignored by the people is held to have fallen into desuetude, and to have no effect. University professors have taught that this only applies to pre-Union statutes, but they do not explain why they make this bland assumption. It is one of the curses of a university that it teaches falsehood with equal persuasion to truth. The man says a Westminster statute cannot fall into desuetude, so it can't.

There is no logic in that view. A Westminster statute can be ignored just as easily as an Edinburgh one. Law, particularly Scots law, is made by the people just as surely as it is made for the people. The sceptre which touches the laws of Scotland, turning dry words into living canons of conduct, is not the royal sceptre, but the acceptance of the law by the Community of the Realm of Scotland. That phrase comes from a great historian, to whom I am indebted for its revival. It is Professor G.W.S. Barrow's phrase. Without the acceptance of the law by the community it is so much mumbo jumbo and incantation. It

199

is witch-doctor's law, not the people's law. Donald Dewar should prepare for Malcolm Rifkind's job by putting the collar bone of a hare through the cartilaginous tissue of his nose. I suspect his laws are going to be more mumbo-jumbo and they will be equally ignored with Malcolm Rifkind's. The bone won't make Donald's laws any more effective, but it will make Donald look more amusing.

When I talk of the ignoring of laws I am referring, of course, to the Poll Tax. That is a splendid example of a Westminster statute being ignored into desuetude. I am making my gesture of ignoring it along with hundreds of thousands of others. I do not regard myself as breaking the law. I am merely invoking the law of the constitution, revived in that case I fought with John MacCormick nearly forty years ago. In time, Westminster, to save its face, will go through the motions of repealing the Poll Tax. But a law passed against the will of the people, is no law of Scotland. That is one of Scotland's great contributions to the constitutional law of the world. We so called Poll Tax rebels are not rebels at all. We are the quiet multitude who, unlike Canute, can turn back the tide, and we are invoking one of the old principles of the law of this realm of Scotland in doing so.

Once started the tide will ebb quickly. Unlike other tides it will not flood again. People have far more common sense than governments. I now make a prophecy. Reform in Scotland will not come with violence. People who take to the streets are yobbos. They soon tire. The little poke of salt in my pocket, will achieve far more than shouting, and carrying it around with me is not a great burden, as I would find attending meetings and shouting in the streets. Yet it is a constant reminder to me of the great principle of the Scottish constitution which Lord Cooper enunciated. 'The principle of the unlimited sovereignty of Parliament is a distinctively English principle which has no counterpart in Scottish constitutional law.' It reminds me that our English masters are

200

not, in law, our masters at all. We have had them on our backs for so long that we are accustomed to them, but that does not make them any more legal. Soon we will throw them off. I give another example of how that may happen, a different example from the Poll Tax.

For many years now a differential transport tax has been imposed in Scotland. It is a silly tax, which holds up the flow of commerce and does little else. I refer to the taxes imposed on anyone getting into and out of Fife at the Forth and Tay bridges. There are other examples, but the Fife example is the best one. Going north and south through Fife every vehicle has to stop at a sort of customs post and pay money. All over Europe customs posts are coming down. What's so special about Fife?

Fife is a lovely county, and Fifers are lovely people. To get the glad-eye from a Fife girl is something smashing, but that is no excuse for Fife having a wee set of customs barriers of its own. It may once have been a kingdom, but today its customs posts are an anachronism. Oh yes, say the Fifers, but the customs posts are imposed by government, not by us. So what? What is significant is not that they are imposed by government, but that Fifers pay at them. Do not blame absurd laws on the dafties at Westminster who impose them. Blame them on the dafties in Fife who support them. Some day soon, I suspect, motorists will start driving through these barriers without paying, and another absurd law will fall into desuetude.

It is not through guns or bombs or any other form of violence that we will get our freedom, as the Scottish Nationalists like to call reform in our ways of Government. It is not even by sending representatives to Westminster. I have long since stopped voting for that silly legislature. It has served its purpose as a place to pension off broken down Labour hacks from local government and the Trade Unions, and as a paddock for quaint old war-horses like my great friend Sir Nicholas Fairbairn to snort and cavort in. The way forward to nationhood is Gandhi's way with a poke of salt. Putting salt on the tail of this foreign Government of Scotland is better than pitched battles.

We never did win many battles in the field, but we aye preserved ourselves by endurance. I have called this book *A Touch of Treason* not merely because it describes my life, but because it describes every Scot. It is part of the fibre of our race, the ringing sound of whose name has gone to the very ends of the earth. Now is the time to make the whole present legislature fall into desuetude. It only needs a wee bit push. We Scots are a pushy lot. A push from the bottom is all that is needed.

Reform from the bottom rather than the top is a romantic idea. It is none the worse for that. My friend Donald Dewar, for him too I name as a friend in this casual comedy of modern Scotland, is a great Westminster man. Recently he called me, 'the last of the great romantics'. It hurt. I would hate to think I was the last. Surely there must be many more. What is life without romance? It is the royal jelly among the virtues. It nourishes the places dogma cannot reach. It makes people aspire. People are romantic. Real people. If we analysed ourselves, Donald Dewar included, we would find that we are far more moved and animated by romance than by self interest. I am. So also is the best in Donald.

Donald, like John Smith, who also is my friend, is consumed with the idea that things can be altered through Westminster. John is different. John is great. He does not have the conventional mind Donald has. He is far and away the most able, and the funniest politician I have known. By funny I mean bubbling with life. He could make a great statesman. Yet so much life is there in John that he wants to go places with an urgency that amounts to a demon within him. And because there are no top places in Scotland he feels he must go elsewhere. John is going to have to watch. He is playing with tragedy. So many of Scotland's fine aspirations have ended in malodorous swamps like the Darien Scheme, and John is living his father's life, not his own. The life, and the very fine life, of an Argyll dominie, cannot be lived at Westminster. At Westminster, to survive you need a 'a genius for compromise', not, as we Scots have, a genius not to compromise, but yet to work together for the common good. If John does not watch very carefully he will end up like James MacKay. Come home, John. Scotland has need of you.

Donald Dewar will laugh at that romantic call. His laughter will not be echoed by John Smith. John has a wider mind. He knows that it is phrases like that that knocked the Berlin Wall down, and took people into the streets from the Baltic to the River Oxus. Patriotism is the romantic notion which Lenin left out of his equation. He was told he was wrong by a wee man from Paisley, who once sat lonely, but not unhappily as a Communist MP. He was Willie Gallagher. He told Lenin that his great state of Soviet Russia would one day all come tumbling down if it was built without love. There's a romantic notion for you. Love. Lenin met his match when he met Willie Gallagher. Willie told Lenin that you cannot neglect the human factor, the romantic factor, the factor that makes people serve best, and most happily, when they serve through their own beloved community. History, which Lenin read more and understood less than Willie Gallagher, is proving Lenin wrong, and the wee man from Paisley right. I know that he told Lenin all that. I had it from Willie Gallagher's own mouth many years ago. Think it over Donald, and perhaps say a wee prayer that before my candle is snuffed out as the last great romantic, a dozen or so may light a torch from my wick and carry on.

There lies another of my failures. The power of song, and the power of poetry, and the power of the drama, and the power of the spoken and written word have moved me greatly. But never the power of prayer. I deny the rationality of

203

human existence. We are, therefore we think. Not, we think, therefore we are. Descartes had it the wrong way round. Yet irrational as I am, I make the absurd and insupportable claim to be moved by rationality. It is not a claim which can logically be advanced by a romantic, and I know that I should be able to offer up a romantic prayer, surely the best of all prayers to make God bend his ear. It would be such a little step from accepting the divinity of thought to accepting the divinity of God, yet it is a step I cannot make. Perhaps I was vaccinated against it in yon church in Paisley. Paralysis seizes me every time I try to take that step. It would be a great comfort if I could. I could blame it all on Him. All the mistakes; all the shoddy things; all the enthusiasms only half lived; all the people hurt, instead of loved. Because love is a greater power than hatred, and hatred hurts both the hated and the hater.

The blame therefore rests on me. God did not make me. I did. Also, I made this book. As a man is, so is his country. As a man is, so is his book; if he tries to be honest, that is, and I have tried to be honest. There are many contradictions in this book, but not nearly as many as there are in my country. For a start, this is a rich land, richest above all in the genius of its people. Yet among us there are some of the poorest people in the world. Poor in spirit, because they are ill-educated. Poor in body because they are ill-fed, and ill-treated. There is no need to have any poor in Scotland. In a rich land like ours, poverty is an artificial creation. It is made by the people, not by the land. In the last ten years it has been created from great wealth, by Mrs Mammon. And we have not had the guts to say, away with you. We can do better by ourselves. We will do it yet.

I deny the doctrine that man enriches the world, by first enriching himself. But what a weariness it is to write that. We Scots have always denied that sterile doctrine. It is not the way we were brought up. It is not the way we bring up our children, and those who do, shame and sin against the whole

204

history of our race. Bread in our mouths is important, but bread in the mouths of people hungrier than we are is more important still. These are brave words. Why don't we speak them more loudly?

That question is easily answered. We have developed thought and doctrines to illuminate the world, but we have been so preoccupied with our big neighbour that we have not bothered to wire ourselves up for sound. We need an amplifier. My voice will still sound as it has always done, girning quietly away. Shortly we will be wired up for sound. We will have our own government, and I can tell you one certain thing about it. Without any peradventure of doubt I will be against it. These are nearly my final words on it.

The only job I want from it is to be ambassador to the Court of St James. I have the fine ancient diplomatic touch.

For some years now my legal colleagues have referred to me as 'The Ancient Mariner', insolent striplings that they are. There may be a change. At home I am now known as 'The Crusty Darling'. Jeannette, Jamie, Stewart and myself have started oyster farming. Oysters have crusty shells. We call ourselves 'The Crusty Darlings'. I'll like my new nickname, if it comes; 'the Crusty Darling'. Give me my oyster shell of quiet. Give me the peace of the West Highlands of Scotland. There, the years will pass over me, but I shall never retire into an oyster shell. I will still be there to maintain the innocence of my fellow citizens, whenever they need my services. My voice has not spoken loudly for Scotland, but whenever it has voiced an opinion, that opinion has aye been on the side of rebellion, if that is the correct word to use for an assertion of the quiet dignity of our own country. My attitude is summed up by MacDiarmid.

> The sons o' freedom drie their weird,
> And huvna loss nor gain.
> For none keeps tryst wi' Scotland
> 'til Scotland's born again.

That time is now upon us. I have not changed, but my country has changed. It recognises itself now. I could never have taken part in the politics of an alien country. I entered manhood with a touch of treason. That is how I felt towards Westminster then. It is not how I feel now. Now I defy Westminster utterly. I defy the right of a vast majority of Englishmen to rule over my country. I defy the right of any Englishman to rule over my country. Westminster, with its immense inbuilt majority of English MPs may be the temporary government of Scotland, but the de jure government, the real government, is the Community of the Realm of Scotland. Ourselves alone.

Do not ask for devolution from Westminster. Westminster has nothing to give us. It is not for England to give us things. It is not even for us Scots to take them. It is for us Scots to create our own political institutions out of our own unbounded and abounding native talent and ability. We are a nation. After three hundred years of foreign government our nationality is unabated. We must create our own political institutions. It is no one's responsibility but our own. Ours, not theirs. Ourselves alone.

Already we are looking around us with a new confidence. Devolution, whatever that may mean, is nearly upon us. The Scottish Grand Committee sits in Edinburgh. At least I think it does. It has been very properly ignored by us Scots, as though it never existed. That is the way to treat Westminster, under whatever guise or disguise it comes. Whatever clothes it wears, we must not even give it a nod of recognition. The only Scotsman Scotland should send to Westminster is an ambassador. Not even a Lord High Commissioner. Ambassadors represent free peoples, and we are a people hewn of an ancient and enduring freedom.

'Look ye into the pit whence ye were dug, and unto the rock from which ye were hewn.' said the prophet Isaiah. Strangers have come to our country, black, white, brown, and yellow among them, but they have not tried to teach us their ways.

Instead they have done us the great honour of adopting ours, and of joining the body politic of Scotland. They are as Scottish as any family who has lived here for two thousand years and more. Only a handful of anglicised Scots disgrace us by aping the ways of the English, just as Mrs Thatcher disgraces the English, and the true spirit of England, by aping the ways of America. When we look at the rock from which we were hewn we need not be ashamed. It is a fine stone and there is plenty of great material left in that quarry, for ourselves and for the world. We will serve the world better when we serve also ourselves.

We are part of world history. Two hundred and nine years ago a handful of American settlers, many Scots among them, defied the greatest power the world had seen since the days of Rome. The old regimes laughed at them and their puny handwritten constitution, a constitution which has endured, with amendments, to this day. Scots had a hand in the writing of it. It is the constitution of the country whose President lives in the White House. With a jest about the White House I draw this book to an end. A jest and a family boast. My family made the White House white, so we did. Before 1812 the White House was not white. It was just a dirty grey. In the War of 1812 my granny's great-uncle Tom set fire to it. He burned down the White House.

When the Americans repaired it they whitewashed it to hide great-uncle Tom's burn marks. But the burn marks keep showing through, just as the nation of Scotland has kept showing through.

If one Scot can make the White House white, five million of us can make our Parliament House a Parliament again. We will see it soon. When the Queen rides to the State opening of the first Scottish Parliament since 1707, I'll be there. See the Queen! See me! I'm the wee man standing in the crowd with his hands in his pockets, and the wry grin on his face. See any Scot. See me.